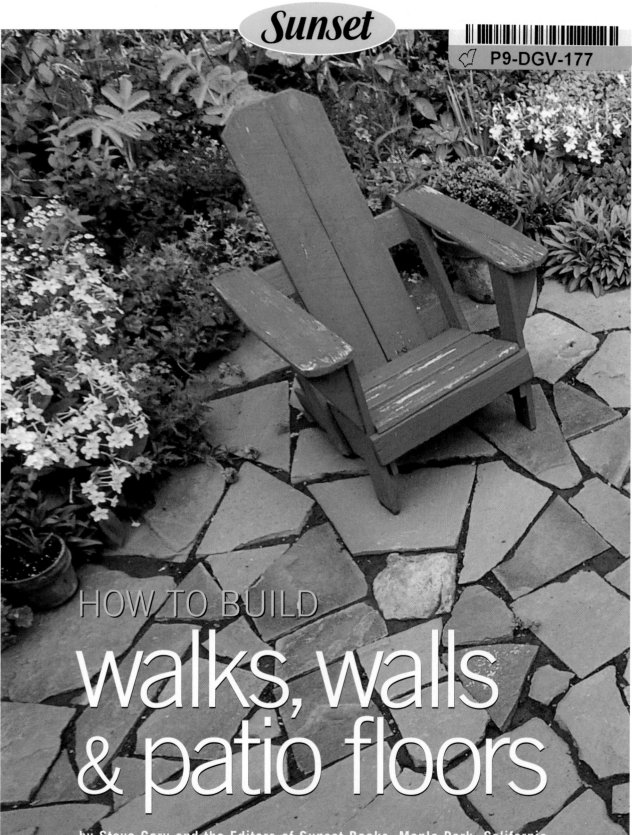

Sunset

HOW TO BUILD
walks, walls
& patio floors

by Steve Cory and the Editors of Sunset Books, Menlo Park, California

SUNSET BOOKS

Vice President & General Manager: Richard A. Smeby
Vice President & Editorial Director: Bob Doyle
Production Director: Lory Day
Director of Operations: Rosann Sutherland
Sales Development Director: Linda Barker
Art Director: Vasken Guiragossian

Staff for this book:
Managing Editor: Bridget Biscotti Bradley
Writer: Steve Cory
Art Director: Amy Gonzalez
Text Editor: Esther Ferington
Photo Editor and Stylist: Ryan Fortini
Principal Photographer: Frank Gaglione
Illustrator: Anthony Davis
Page Production: Linda M. Bouchard
Production Coordinator: Danielle Javier
Proofreader: Carol Boker
Indexer: Nanette Cardon

Cover: Photography by Susan A. Roth. Garden Design by Duncan Callicot.

For additional copies of *How to Build Walks, Walls & Patio Floors* or any other Sunset book, call 1-800-526-5111 or visit us at www.sunset.com.

contents

Chapter One

planning

Masonry structures are almost magical in their ability to lend both solidity and charm to a landscape at the same time. With masonry as a design element, you can never go far wrong: rough stones, classic bricks, cut tiles, adobe blocks, and modern concrete pavers can complement almost any style of architecture, and are equally suited to small yards and large expanses.

This book concentrates on projects that are well within the reach of a motivated do-it-yourselfer. You'll find much of the work physically challenging because masonry units are heavy. So take it slowly, and enlist help. However, none of the tasks requires special skills. If you follow the steps described in this book, you can achieve outdoor structures that are every bit as durable and beautiful as those installed by a pro.

This section introduces you to most of the materials used for patios, walks, and walls. The following section, on pages 25–40, describes the process of laying out, excavating, and installing edging—all of which must be done prior to installing a paver or concrete patio. Pages 41–78 give instructions for the most popular outdoor masonry projects—laying bricks, stones, or pavers in sand or tamped soil. On pages 79–98, you'll find directions for the most challenging project, pouring concrete for a patio, walk, or footing. That section also shows several ways to spruce up an existing concrete slab or wall. Finally, pages 99–125 tackle the task of building modest walls out of brick or stone.

brick

Traditional and versatile, brick has long been a popular choice for patios and walkways. The rustic charm of baked and weathered clay is at home in any landscape. Natural brick is not as strong and weather-resistant as concrete pavers, but if you choose the right type, a brick patio or wall can last for centuries with little maintenance.

BRICK OPTIONS

Brick is made from clay fired in a kiln; the higher the heat, the stronger the brick. Years ago bricks were molded by hand, but today the clay is extruded or pushed through a die and cut to size after the clay has air-dried.

Brick offers a broad palette of color, style, and texture. You will find a few common examples below. Check with your local suppliers to find these and other unique products.

Be aware that brick may change in appearance over time. For instance, the surface of a porous brick eventually acquires a patina, giving it a soft, polished look.

For a dressy look, such as the patio shown on the opposite page, a neat pattern of smooth, regular brick has a classic appeal.

The weathered look of salvaged brick in a meandering pattern, shown above, offers a more casual and relaxed feeling.

Especially in an area with freezing winters, many bricks that survive on walls do not survive as patio pavers, where they are subject to much more pressure. Buy bricks rated strong enough for paving. Use bricks rated SX if your ground freezes; use bricks that are rated MX only in a warm climate. Consult with your dealer to make sure the brick you buy will last.

DESIGNING A BRICK PATIO

The brick pattern you choose will define the character of a patio or wall almost as much as the specific type of brick. See page 52 for patio patterns.

Edge a brick patio with large timbers or 2× lumber for a less formal look. If you use plastic or metal ribbon edging, the bricks can meet the lawn or another surface seamlessly.

Install brick pavers tight against each other on a bed of gravel and sand. Or mortar spaced-apart bricks onto a stable concrete slab, and fill the joints with mortar (see page 98).

concrete pavers

Perhaps remembering the oil-stained garage floors of their youth, many people are skeptical about concrete as a material for the beautification of home or landscape. But recent innovations have cast colored concrete in a variety of attractive small forms. Today's concrete pavers are made from a dense formula of concrete that is pressure-formed in machines. They withstand all the elements and provide good choices in any area of the country. Inexpensive concrete pavers can be manufactured to resemble brick, tile, or stone, and they can be installed the same way.

Often pavers are easier to install than bricks because they are uniform in size. Many pavers interlock neatly without joints and form a surface that is smooth, solid, and suitable for heavy traffic (see page 53). Non-interlocking pavers can be arranged with tight joints for a neat seamless look, or with open joints that sprout grass for a more casual look.

CHOOSING CONCRETE PAVERS

Interlocking pavers in shades of pink, gray, tan, or reddish brown are inexpensive and easy to find. Pavers that duplicate the look of stone or adobe are more expensive and, as a result, may need to be special-ordered. When you select your pavers, take note that better-quality pavers have a uniform color throughout and not just on the surface, so that any chips are less noticeable.

Immerse yourself in the paver possibilities, browsing the aisles at local garden supply centers. Paver shapes include circles, rectangles, hexagons, triangles, and a variety of more complex interlocking patterns, some of which nicely mimic old-fashioned cobblestone.

Circular Paver Ensemble

In the days before concrete pavers, creating a circular patio of brick was a labor-intensive project involving a lot of cutting. Now, concrete pavers that resemble brick are available in all the special-size pieces needed for the inner section of a circle pattern, and no cutting is needed.

adobe

west makes them hard to find in the Midwest and Northeast.

Adobe blocks are fairly massive. The most common sizes are 4 by 8 by 16 and 4 by 8 by 8. Blocks range in weight from 12 to 45 pounds. Installing them is a good workout.

Because adobe blocks or pavers are large, they tend to be used in generous, open garden spaces. The blocks vary slightly in size, so it's best to avoid patterns that call for a tight fit. Running bond, jack-on-jack, and basketweave patterns (see page 52) work well; the latter two require no cutting. Laid in sand with 1-inch-wide joints—filled with either sand or low-growing ground cover and moss—an informal adobe patio or walkway offers a warm, inviting quality that is hard to rival.

Big slabs of dried clay from the Southwest have long been stacked to form walls or used as pavers for patios. Adobe has been used with good results for centuries. It has been made mainly from soil from the Southwest mixed with straw and water and left to dry in the sun.

Traditional adobe wore down under the stress of heat and rain and needed an occasional recoating of adobe plaster. Today, asphalt emulsion or Portland cement is added to the mix to improve stability, and sometimes a hydraulic compressor speeds up the hardening process. Adobe units made with asphalt are darker in color; those made with Portland cement resemble the traditional mud and straw bricks.

Today's adobe units hold up well in any weather, even cold climates, although the expense of shipping them outside the South-

tile

Handmade Mexican saltillo, rustic terra cotta, glazed or unglazed ceramic, or hand-painted accent tiles—the array of tile choices is a sumptuous palette. Tile out of doors can be as stunning as it is indoors. But there are some logistical points to consider:

- Tile costs more than brick or concrete pavers.
- Installation requirements are more stringent. Tile needs to be installed over a perfectly level surface. The well-tamped bed of sand that works for brick, stone, or concrete pavers will cause thin tiles to crack, even under normal traffic conditions. In most cases, tile must be set in thinset mortar on top of a solid concrete slab.
- Maintenance requirements can be higher. You need to protect unglazed tile with a sealer when it is first installed, and reapply the sealer periodically.
- Glazed tile, when wet, is usually too slippery for an outdoor floor surface, and some unglazed tile is, too. In addition, the glaze can give off harsh reflections of sunlight. Glazed tile works best for occasional accents.
- Porous tile attracts mildew and moss in cool, wet climates, and stains easily.

If you'd like to use tile in your landscape, it's a good idea to seek local advice to find out which varieties work best in your area. Also be sure to read all the fine print supplied by the manufacturer. The strength and surface properties of a tile depend on a combination of the clay and the firing process. Tile that is fired at low temperatures tends to be softer and less dense, with a more porous surface; tile fired at higher temperatures is denser, with a slicker, glasslike surface.

If the tiles you choose are ¾ inch or thicker and very strong you may try laying them over a bed of smooth and level sand. A more stable installation on a concrete slab is preferable. See pages 80–87 for instructions on pouring a new concrete slab, and pages 96–97 for tiling over existing concrete.

stone paths and patios

Stone can often be expensive, especially if it's not native to the area where you live. But it blends beautifully with any landscape, and is likely to tie everything together in your yard.

Rough and irregular slabs of stone artfully placed in a landscape lend an appealing casual look that never goes out of style. The irregular surface provides good traction, making this type of stone popular for paths, but less desirable for chairs and tables or for wheelchairs or wheeled toys—a consideration for patios.

Marble and granite are the hardest stones. Sandstone, limestone, and other sedimentary stones are more porous and usually have a chalky or gritty texture.

FLAGSTONE

Flagstone is a loose term that refers to any large flat stone 1 to 4 inches thick. Most flagstones are produced by splitting, but some are cut to thickness. Stones vary by region and by supplier. Stoneyards will offer pallets of various types of flagstone. The yard may allow you to choose stones one by one, or you may have to buy a large pallet and have it delivered.

Flagstone is available in shades of gray, tan, and brownish red and a variety of surface textures. In some cases, a single pallet contains stones of different colors and textures. Quartzite and some slates can be slippery in frosty weather.

You can place flagstone on top of stable soil to quickly create a path or patio (see pages 56–57), or you can set flagstone in a bed of sand for greater stability. In either case, fill the joints with your choice of plants, sand, or fine gravel. For a more formal look, set flagstones on a concrete slab and mortar them into place. If you take your time selecting stones and piecing them together, you can create a fairly level surface, but you might have a hard time scooting a chair over it.

SLATE

Slate is a dense, smooth metamorphic rock with a fine grain available in a range of colors.

IRISH LINEN FLAGSTONE

It is often used for interior floors. For outdoor floors, it should be used only in mild climates. It is available in tiles or as randomly cut stone. Because the real thing is so expensive, imitation slate is also available.

STONE TILE

Tiles made from stone have smooth surfaces and pleasant variations in color. Some are cut as precisely as regular tile in square or rectangular shapes; others are hand-cut and have random widths and thicknesses. Laid in mortar with very thin grout lines, they lend warmth and formality to a floor surface. Stones often used as tiles include slate, granite, sandstone, and quartzite.

Check with the supplier about a stone tile's suitability for outdoor use. Some may be slippery when wet. Slate and quartzite can be slippery in frosty weather. Some may be porous and prone to stain, which may be a problem for a patio eating area.

MARIPOSA SLATE

BOQUET CANYON FLAGSTONE

BUFF ARIZONA FLAGSTONE

THREE RIVERS FLAGSTONE

LILAC KASHMIR SLATE

FERNLEAF SLATE

GRAY SLATE

loose materials

Loose materials offer an easy, economical option for patios and walkways. With a little bit of imagination, the result can be practical and inviting.

CHOOSING LOOSE MATERIALS

A home center typically sells loose materials in bags suitable for small projects. At a stoneyard or building materials supplier, you may find bins of loose materials, which you can shovel into your pickup or have delivered—an easier and less expensive option for larger projects.

Among the more popular loose materials are quartz pebbles, redrock, decomposed granite chips, and river rocks. Colors include white, gray, tan, and red. Like natural stone, these materials naturally complement foliage and natural wood.

Many organic materials, such as shredded bark and redwood or cypress chips, are surprisingly long-lived. They can form a cushioned floor for children's play areas.

Any loose material provides good drainage; water can soak right through. If water tends to puddle at the edge of a patio, for instance, you may choose to dig a trench there and fill it with pebbles or crushed stone.

Pebbles, large gravel, and organic materials will stay loose, meaning they are not practical for heavy traffic areas. Crushed granite and other small-grained materials, however, are more compactible. After running a drum roller over one of these, you will have a path that is fairly hard and smooth (see page 75).

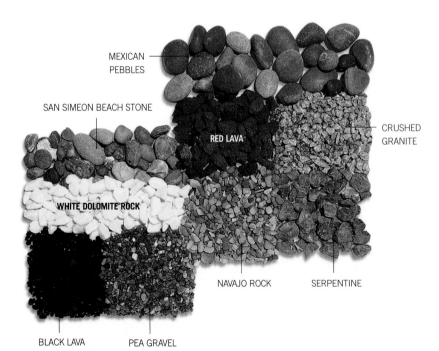

MEXICAN PEBBLES

SAN SIMEON BEACH STONE

RED LAVA

CRUSHED GRANITE

WHITE DOLOMITE ROCK

NAVAJO ROCK

SERPENTINE

BLACK LAVA

PEA GRAVEL

DESIGNING WITH LOOSE MATERIALS

Loose materials work best in small areas; a large gravel or pebble patio is impractical. Use loose materials for a path, a border around a patio or deck, or a transition between a patio and a garden.

The exception is a Japanese garden, which typically includes a large area covered with pebbles or sand, perhaps with pavers or flagstones scattered around.

Take home samples of loose materials, as you would paint chips, and scatter them on the ground to see how they look. Keep in mind that the color will become more intense when spread over a large area.

stone walls

Here, short retaining walls made of semidressed stone form two meandering terraces. Stacked flagstones (right) make a casual retaining wall. An ashlar garden wall (below, right) is only slightly more formal.

BOQUET CANYON ASHLAR BLEND

BOQUET CANYON ASHLAR BLEND

RED ARIZONA FLAGSTONE

THREE RIVERS FLAGSTONE

THREE RIVERS FLAGSTONE

BOQUET CANYON FLAGSTONE

Some of the most ancient human structures are walls made of stone. A wall that you build of natural stone today will quickly attain an antique look, especially if foliage grows in its joints.

CHOOSING BUILDING STONE

You may be able to find stones lying around, perhaps partially buried, right on your property. Or stone of all sorts may be rare in your area, making a stone wall something of a luxury. Visit a stoneyard or building materials supplier to check your options.

Stone colors range from nearly pure white to shades of gray, brown, yellow, and red. Don't be afraid to mix hues in a single project; it's almost impossible to make a bad color choice when it comes to natural stone.

A supplier may list a variety of categories, but basically four types of stone are available. "Rubble" is uncut stone, usually with rounded edges. It is usually the cheapest option, but is very difficult to work with. Use it for accent boulders, but don't try to build a boulder wall unless you have some experienced help. Flagstone is any fairly thin and flat stone. "Semi-dressed stone," such as cobblestone, has

been roughly shaped. It can be stacked to form a firm wall, though you may need to experiment and adjust quite a bit as you work. "Ashlar" is fully trimmed stone that is almost as easy to lay as brick (right).

DESIGNING STONE WALLS

Use stone to build a decorative garden wall or to make a retaining wall that holds soil in place.

A mortared stone wall (see pages 122–123) must be laid on top of a firm concrete footing (see pages 88–89) or the joints will crack. In an area with freezing winters, the footing must extend below the frost line. A dry stone wall (see pages 120–121) can be laid on a bed of gravel, even in areas with freezing winters.

This book shows how to build low, modest stone walls. Anything taller than 4 feet is a major project calling for lots of heavy lifting.

brick and block walls

It takes experience to quickly lay a brick or block wall that is straight and level. However, a homeowner with time and patience can tackle a small project. Pages 110–111 teach the basics of masonry wall construction.

CHOOSING WALL BRICK

Common brick, often called building or standard brick, comes rough and somewhat irregular in shape, and ranges in color from light tan to deep reddish brown.

Facing brick is generally more regular in shape, but may have a rough, decorative surface on the side that faces outward for a wall. Wire-cut brick has vertical stripes; rough facing brick has a cracked appearance. Holes in the brick help the mortar adhere when building a wall. A "frogged" brick

Natural brick, laid in a running bond pattern, creates this sturdy, attractive wall. The well-manicured landscape shown below, with stairs, stepping-stones, raised beds, and a three-tiered retaining wall, proves you can never have too much brick.

has an indentation that often features a manufacturer's stamp.

Glazed brick has a smooth, polished side. It is expensive, but you may like its gleaming appearance. Used brick (which may be cheap or expensive, depending on where you live) instantly creates an antique wall or patio. Some manufacturers produce concrete pavers that are made to look like used bricks.

See page 112 for wall bond patterns. You can cap a brick wall with more brick, but it also looks great abutting other surfaces. Consider edging a concrete patio with a short brick wall or using a limestone cap.

CHOOSING CONCRETE BLOCK

The large size of concrete blocks—8 by 8 by 16 inches is standard—makes for rapid progress in building. To build a low block wall, follow the steps for building with brick. Consult with a pro before tackling a block wall that is over 4 feet high, or that must serve as a retaining wall.

Some decorative blocks can resemble cut stone or even adobe. Screen or grille blocks, like the one at right, form patterned screen walls that admit light and air while providing some privacy.

To construct a retaining wall quickly, use stackable concrete retaining blocks (see pages 108–109).

A stuccoed block wall takes fanciful turns to retain soil for a large sloped garden bed.

making a plan

Enclosing walls and a decorative window give this patio the feel of an outdoor room. However, the walls are low and the patio is generously sized, so the feel is anything but confined.

A patio, path, or wall can help transform a ho-hum yard into an inviting setting for entertaining, relaxing, and dining. To do this successfully, however, outdoor structures must be planned carefully, so they both enhance the look of your surroundings and suit your needs. This book concentrates on the nitty-gritty of building walks, walls, and patio floors; these two pages offer only general planning advice. For more ideas, see Sunset's *Ideas for Great Patios and Decks* and *Complete Patio Book.*

FROM DREAM TO PLAN

Start the planning process by developing a wish list. How would you like to use your yard? What sort of atmosphere would you like to create? Then compare your dream with present reality. Which aspects of your yard do you like, and which would you change? Aim for a design that maximizes the yard's assets and makes the most of its liabilities. For instance, a sloped lawn is difficult to use, but offers the possibility of two or more patios on different levels, retaining walls and

steps. A small, flat yard with too-close neighbors can be transformed into a cozy retreat by installing a patio, walls, and large plants. If you have a long walk to the garbage, build an attractive path.

PRACTICAL CONSIDERATIONS

Realistically assess how you will use your yard. If you entertain often with sit-down meals, plan a space to accommodate a large table with chairs. If you only entertain occasionally, or if scattered-site dining is more to your liking, then you do not need a single large space.

Set patio furniture—table with chairs, as well as lounging chairs—out on the lawn. Have your family experiment to find the most comfortable arrangement, then plan the contours of a patio and the location of any walls.

As a general rule, a dining area for six people should be at least 12 feet square. For barbecuing, allow a space that is about 6 feet by 8 feet. A lounge chair will occupy a space of about 4 feet by 8 feet. Plan for 3-foot-wide pathways that do not run through areas where people will be sitting.

DRAWING A PLAN

When planning small or large landscapes, it helps to draw out the plans. First, a bubble sketch: Make a scale drawing of the site;

include trees and other plants, and copy it several times. Roughly sketch in bubble-shaped areas that define activities and describe the structures. Experiment with different ideas until you have a general plan.

Second, draw a plan view. This is an aerial view of the site. Be as specific as possible. Measure carefully, and perhaps even draw the patio bricks to scale. Include accessories such as lawn furniture and flower pots. This drawing will give you a realistic idea of the

available space and will help you estimate the quantity of materials that will be needed.

Third, make detail drawings from a side, or elevation, view. These get into the nuts and bolts of the installation. Include substrate materials and drainage solutions.

Once your plans are final and the drawings complete, make an exhaustive materials list; it will save you time in the long run. If possible, ask a building inspector or landscape designer to check your plans before construction begins.

DETAIL VIEW

$4 \times 8 \times 2$ PAVERS

$1\frac{1}{2}$" SAND

4×4 EDGING

REBAR

3" COMPACTIBLE GRAVEL

PLAN VIEW

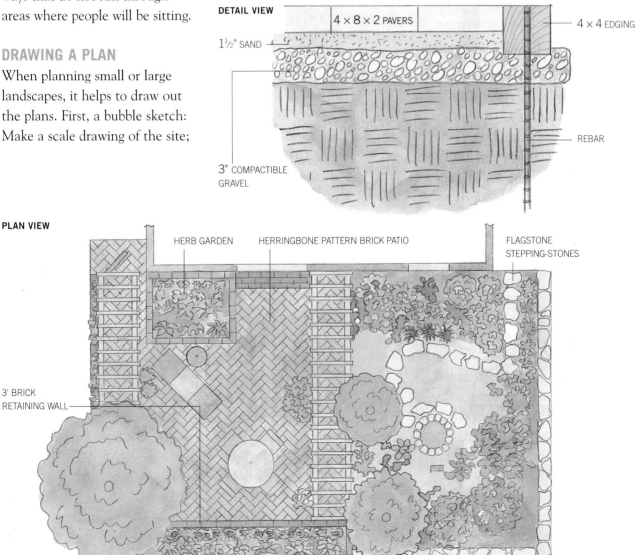

HERB GARDEN HERRINGBONE PATTERN BRICK PATIO FLAGSTONE STEPPING-STONES

3' BRICK RETAINING WALL

TOOLS FOR WORKING WITH CONCRETE

To lay out and excavate for a concrete slab, use the tools shown on page 22. Pouring and smoothing the concrete calls for special tools. If you will be using these tools only once, consider renting rather than purchasing them. Do not pour a slab without these tools, however, or you could end up with a very unattractive finish that cannot be redeemed.

Once the concrete has been very roughly leveled with a 2 × 4 screed, you'll need several tools to produce a progressively smoother surface. For the first round, use a darby (A) for a narrow slab. If a darby will not reach all the way across, use a bull float (B).

For the next round, use a wooden float (C) or a magnesium float (D) to produce a somewhat smooth surface. At this point, you may choose to brush the surface with a stiff broom, for a skid-resistant finish. To produce a very smooth surface, go over the surface with a steel trowel (E). Be aware, however, that it takes a good deal of practice before you can use a steel trowel successfully.

Use an edger (F) to round the edges of a slab, and a jointer (G) to make control joints in the middle.

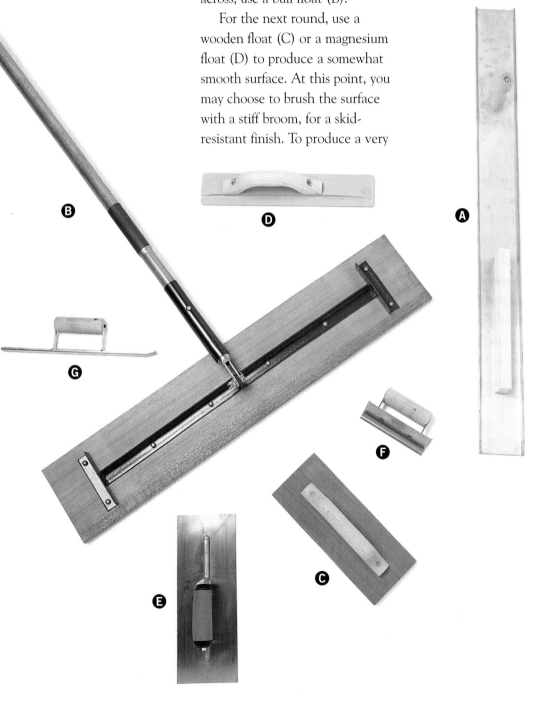

excavation and edging

Before installing any patio surface—whether brick, concrete paver, flagstone, or poured concrete—you may need to take three steps to prepare the site. First, lay out an outline of the future patio and determine the patio's height; it should slope gently away from the house, and the edge that runs parallel to the house should be level. Second, you must excavate the area to the correct depth, so that the finished surface will be an inch or so above grade. And third, you need to install edgings—permanent in the case of a brick or paver patio and temporary in the case of a concrete slab. Once these steps have been completed, you will be ready to lay a brick or paver patio (see pages 41–78), or to pour a concrete slab (see pages 79–98).

laying out for a patio

Use spray paint or mason's line strung between stakes to mark the general outline of your proposed patio, keeping in mind the activity areas as described on page 21. Then use the procedures on these pages to precisely mark the perimeter of the patio.

THE ORDER OF WORK

To prepare for a patio of bricks or pavers laid in sand, it is usually best to follow these steps:

- Lay out the perimeter using the techniques shown on this page.
- Dig up and remove all sod and any plants inside the perimeter.
- Install the edgings, correctly sloped when they are perpendicular to the house and level when they are parallel to the house, so they can act as guides for the height of the patio.

- String a grid of guide lines across the edgings and then excavate the interior of the patio to the correct depth.

If the patio area receives plenty of rain, or if it is larger than 500 square feet, you may need to install a drainage trench, or even a dry well or catch basin. Usually this is done before putting in the edgings; see pages 36–37.

If you plan to use a decorative edging that is uneven or not at the same level as the patio (see page 40), it's probably easiest to install the patio surface first, using temporary guides, and then install the edging.

To excavate for a concrete slab, follow the same steps, but install temporary 2 × 4 edging, which will be removed when the concrete hardens.

CHECKING FOR SQUARE

To lay out a rectangular patio, construct two batterboards for each outside corner. (Usually, you do not need them for the corners where the patio abuts the house.) At each corner, pound two batterboards about 2 feet beyond the estimated location of the corner, facing in either direction.

Tightly stretch lines around the perimeter as shown (opposite page). The strings should be close to the ground but should not touch the ground at any point.

To check for square, mark a spot on the house exactly 6 feet from the corner. Use a piece of tape to mark the adjacent string at precisely 8 feet from the corner. Measure the diagonal distance between the two marks; if it is precisely 10 feet, then the corner is square. If necessary, move the string to one side or the other until the diagonal is exactly 10 feet. Check the other corners in the same way. If the patio is large, follow the same method using multiples of 6, 8, and 10, such as 12, 16, and 20, or 18, 24, and 30.

To double-check, measure the patio's diagonals from corner to corner; they should be the same length. Also check that the patio is the same width at either end.

To make a batterboard, attach a 24" long 1 × 2 to two 1 × 2 stakes. Make the stakes about 18" long, or longer or shorter if ground is unusually soft or hard.

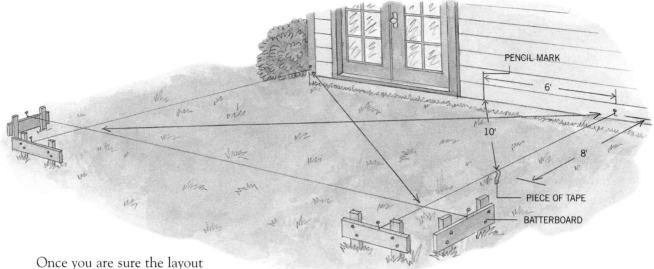

PENCIL MARK

6'

10'

8'

PIECE OF TAPE

BATTERBOARD

Once you are sure the layout is correct, drive a nail or screw at the correct spot on each batterboard, so you can replace the line if it gets bumped out of position.

MARKING A CURVE

To mark the ground for a curve, lay a garden hose on the ground in the desired shape. Pour sand over the hose all along its length. When you pick up the hose, you will have a clear outline of the desired curve.

PLUMB BOB

SAND

MARKING A CORNER

Dangle a plumb bob (or a chalk line) so that its string line nearly touches the intersection of two layout lines and the weight is nearly resting on the ground. Mark the patio corner by driving a stake into the ground.

removing sod and excavating for the edging

Any organic matter, such as sod, plants, or topsoil with a strong mulch content, must be removed prior to installing a patio. Otherwise, the material will eventually decompose and leave cavities, causing the patio to sink.

If there is a tree nearby, you'll also need to cut away any roots that come within a foot or so of the surface. Removing large roots will probably damage the tree, however, and the tree may also send new roots in the same direction within a few years. Even if a tree's roots do not yet reach into the patio area, they may travel there in the near future; consult with a nursery to find out. If you do not wish to remove a tree that impinges on the patio, consider installing a loose-material surface (see pages 74–75).

DETERMINING WHERE TO CUT THE SOD

It's difficult to cut sod in a precise straight line, so usually it's best to cut the sod 1 or 2 inches outside the line where the edging will go. That makes it easier to create a solid and level subsurface for the edging. It is not difficult to backfill the resulting space with soil and sod.

REMOVING SOD

For a small patio, dig up sod with a square shovel. First cut a line around the perimeter, holding the shovel blade straight vertically.

Slice a parallel line about 18 inches inside the patio, then undercut the sod between the two lines, and roll it up as you remove it (above). Depending on your type of sod, you may increase or decrease the width of the rolls.

For a larger patio, consider renting a sod cutter. This tool makes sod cutting easier (though it's still hard work) and simplifies the task of slicing straight lines—which will make it easier to excavate for the edging.

MEASURING FOR LEVEL AND SLOPE

As a general rule, a patio should slope down and away from the house at the rate of $\frac{1}{4}$ inch per foot; where it is parallel to the house, the patio should be level. On the house, mark a level reference line to indicate the finished height of the patio—about 1 inch below the bottom of the door's threshold. From that line, string reference lines that are either level or correctly sloped for the

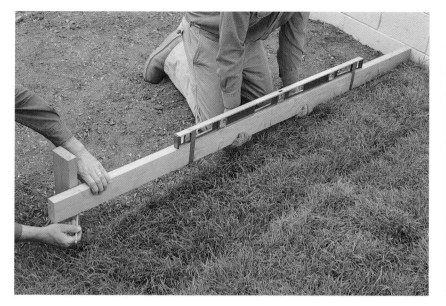

other three sides. The reference lines should be at the finish height of the edging. Firmly drive stakes at each corner for attaching string lines.

If the patio is 16 feet or less in width, check for level by placing a carpenter's level on a long, straight board. To measure for level over a long distance, use a line level. Stretch a line very taut, and place the level in the center of the run. Check the bubble; then reverse the level. If the bubble is in the same place, the level is accurate; if not, either bend the metal tabs (if any) to make it accurate or buy a new level. For maximum accuracy, buy or rent a water level (above left) and follow the manufacturer's instructions.

To position a reference line for a side that slopes, mark the stake for level; then measure down ¼ inch per linear foot and attach the string line at that point (above right). The line may get bumped as you work, so double-check from time to time.

EXCAVATING A TRENCH

Determine how deep the trench needs to be. For most edgings, the trench should be 3 to 5 inches deeper than the edging material, to accommodate a base of gravel and sand. Dig with a square shovel, scraping the bottom of the trench rather than digging downward, so you do not disturb the soil (below).

Leave One Side Open

To minimize the need to cut patio pavers, don't install one side of the edging. Instead, temporarily install a 2 x 4 to use as a height guide. Once you have laid all or most of the patio, you can install the final section of edging against the last row of full-size pavers (see step 11 on page 61).

paver edging

Typically, this type of edging uses the same paving material as the patio surface, though you could use a contrasting material.

LAYING UPRIGHT EDGING PAVERS

It is important to anchor the edging firmly so it can keep the patio pavers from wandering. Installing the edging units as shown—upright, with the thickness rather than the width facing the patio—orients the pavers for the greatest stability. Depending on local soil conditions, you may choose to set such "soldiers" in wet mortar; consult with a local paving contractor.

1 Establish a Firm Base
Measuring from the reference line (see page 28), dig a trench that is 4 inches deeper than the height of the pavers. Shovel in 3 inches of gravel, and tamp it firm with a hand tamper or a piece of 4 × 4. To make a screed guide, cut a piece of 2 × 6 to the same length as the pavers. Pour sand over the gravel, and scrape across the sand with the guide, so that the sand is the height of one paver below the reference line. Spray the sand with a fine mist of water until it is thoroughly wet. Add more sand and screed again.

2 Set the Bricks
Place each paver so its outside corner comes within ⅛ inch of the reference line. After you have installed 4 feet or so, lay a straight board on top and tap it to form a smooth, even surface.

3 Backfill
Stake a straight 2 × 4 against the inside, patio edge of the pavers. Backfill with soil and tamp gently; you will tamp the soil more firmly after installing the patio pavers.

PAVER-ON-CONCRETE EDGING

To establish a firmer surface, install a concrete footing and lay the pavers in mortar on top. With this method, it is common to lay the pavers on their sides.

Install the footing below the reference line (that is, the planned top surface of the finished patio) by the thickness of one paver plus ¼ inch. See pages 88–89 for instructions on pouring a footing. The footing does not need to extend below the frost line, but it should be at least 1 foot thick and 6 inches wider than the edging pavers.

Allow the footing to set for a couple of days. Trowel mortar onto the concrete, and set the bricks, using the reference line and a straight board to ensure an even surface that is either level or sloped correctly . Also stake a straight board against the inside patio edge to ensure a straight line.

Turning a Curve on Paver Edging

Because you can't string a curved line, stake a benderboard as a guide for a curved edge; see page 33. The joints between the pavers will be slightly wider on the outside of the curve.

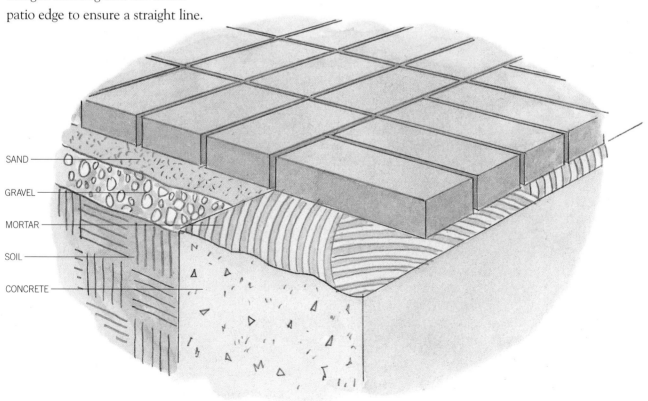

SAND

GRAVEL

MORTAR

SOIL

CONCRETE

wood edging

Choose wood that is proven to withstand ground contact in your area. The dark heartwood of redwood works well, but it is expensive. Pressure-treated lumber rated "ground contact" is more durable and less costly.

Select boards carefully. They should be straight and free of large knots. If you cut a board, apply two or more coats of sealer to the cut end.

TWO-BY EDGING

Wood edging made of 2 × 4 or 2 × 6 lumber is plenty strong, as long as you support it with 2 × 4 stakes every two feet or so. Dig a trench 4 to 5 inches wide, so there will be room for the 2× edging and the stakes, plus an extra inch or two. Make the trench deep enough to place 2 to 3 inches of gravel under the boards. Shovel gravel into the trench and tamp it firm.

1 Check the Board for Level and Straightness

Cut the edging boards to length and lay them on top of the gravel, so that the inside corners are about ¼ inch away from the layout lines. Tap the boards down into the gravel if necessary. You may need to dig away or add gravel in order to support the boards at all points.

2 Drive Stakes

Cut stakes out of pressure-treated 2 × 4s. The pointed tips should be about 4 inches long. The length of the stakes depends on soil conditions; it should take some effort to drive them all the way in but not be so difficult that you split the stakes. You may choose metal stakes. Using a scrap of 2× lumber to keep from splitting the stakes, drive them about 1½ inches below the top of the edging boards.

3 Attach with Screws and Backfill

Check again that the edging is straight and aligned with the layout lines. From the inside of the excavation, drive two 2½-inch rust-resistant deck screws through the edging and into each stake. Shovel 2 inches of gravel into the trench; then fill with soil and lightly tamp with a 2 × 4; take care not to nudge the edging out of alignment. After the patio is laid, you will tamp the soil more firmly.

CURVED WOOD EDGING

If curved edging butts against straight 2× lumber, you will want the curved edging to be 1½ inches thick to match the straight lumber. For gentle curves, use two thicknesses of 1 × 4 or 1 × 6. Redwood benderboard, which is ⅜ to ½ inch thick, makes tighter bends but may be difficult to find in some areas. A lumberyard may rip-cut benderboard pieces out of 2 × 4s or 2 × 6s for a modest price.

Because you cannot accurately measure the length of a curve, install curved wood edging using pieces that are longer than you need. Then cut one or more ends to length after the benderboard is firmly staked in place.

1 Bend the Boards into Position
Drive stakes, 1½ inches below the top of the edging, at the beginning and end of a curved run, on the outside of the bender-board (that is, the side outside the patio). Working with a helper, bend the board to the desired shape. Drive temporary stakes along the inside of the boards to hold them in place. Attach the benderboard pieces to one stake only by drilling pilot holes and driving deck screws.

2 Install and Attach Permanent Stakes
Use a carpenter's level to check that the benderboards are level or correctly sloped. Every 2 feet or so, drive a permanent stake on the outside of the benderboards, so its top is 1½ inches below the top of the benderboard. Drill pilot holes and drive deck screws to attach the benderboards to the permanent stakes; then remove the temporary stakes.

3 Cut the Ends
Once the pieces are secured to the stakes, use an angle square or a framing square to draw a cutoff line, at the point where the patio edging becomes straight. Cut the benderboards using a handsaw or a reciprocating saw.

excavating and adding gravel

Once sod is removed from a patio site, all organic matter must be removed as well. Large roots from a nearby tree will lift a patio up if they continue to grow, and can cause depressions if they die and rot. Either turn of events can create waves in a paver patio or cracks in a concrete slab. As a general rule of thumb, all visible roots larger than $\frac{1}{2}$ inch in diameter should be cut away and removed. To be safe, however, if there is any tree within 10 feet of the patio consult with a nursery to find out how fast the tree will grow and whether its roots tend to grow near the surface. If you suspect that roots will be a problem, consider installing a loose-material path or patio (see pages 74–75).

The goal of excavating is to remove all soil to a depth that will accommodate gravel, sand, and surface material, and to dig no further. A patio substrate should rest on undisturbed soil, which is firmer than soil that has been dug up and replaced.

Determine how deep the excavation should be—that is, the thickness of the total patio, including the gravel and sand substrate. For a brick or paver patio, a typical installation calls for 2 to 3 inches of gravel, plus $1\frac{1}{2}$ inches of sand, plus the thickness of the pavers. For a concrete slab, it is common to have 3 inches of gravel plus 3 inches of concrete. However, local conditions may change these numbers quite a bit; consult with a contractor or your local building department to see how things are usually done in your area.

EXCAVATE THE INTERIOR

Once you are sure that the edging is at the correct height all around, use it as a guide for the excavation depth. Attach a grid of mason's lines to the edging, spacing the lines 4 to 5 feet apart in both directions (shown left). If the edging is wood, simply drive nails or screws and tie the strings to them. If you have brick edging, drive stakes a foot or two outside the patio and tie the strings to the stakes so that the lines rest on top of the bricks. Pull the lines very taut.

To create an easy-to-use depth gauge, wrap a piece of duct tape around the handle of a shovel at the correct depth, or mark a piece of scrap lumber.

Dig first with a pointed shovel, taking care not to dig below the

finished depth of the excavation. Then use a square shovel to scrape the bottom (right). Aim for a fairly smooth and consistent bottom surface.

If you accidentally dig more than 2 inches too deep in one spot, fill the hole with soil, tamp firmly with a 2 × 4, and repeat the process until you reach the correct height.

ADD AND TAMP GRAVEL

Order compactible gravel, made to serve as a substrate for a paver patio or concrete slab. To figure how much you need in cubic yards, see pages 80–81, or ask your supplier.

Have the gravel delivered by truck. If possible, ask the supplier to dump the gravel directly into the excavated area. If not, you may have to use wheelbarrows; see page 83.

Rent a vibrating plate compactor an hour or two before the gravel will be delivered, so you can power tamp the soil first, and then the gravel. You may also want to rent this machine to tamp the finished paver surface (see page 61).

Spread the gravel first with shovels; then rake it to achieve an even depth. You can tamp a small area by hand using a 4 × 4 or a hand tamper, but a vibrating plate compactor tamps much more firmly, virtually assuring a patio surface free of buckles and cracks for years. Run the compactor over the surface several times to make the gravel surface as hard and solid as possible.

decorative edgings

Consider edging your patio with unusual materials, which not only add interest but also clearly define the patio as an outdoor room.

Decorative edgings are often uneven, and so cannot be used as a guide for excavating (see pages 38–39). They also cannot be counted on to form a solid frame to hold pavers in place. Build the patio first, using an unobtrusive plastic or metal edging. Then add the decorative edging.

Some decorative edgings make it difficult to mow the lawn. Others can be set an inch below grade, so you can run the lawn mower over them.

Large boulders, like the ones shown at left, can simply be set in shallow holes. Depending on their size, you may need to hire a company to deliver and set them in place. Flagstone can be laid around the edge in well-tamped soil (see pages 56–57). Fill the joints with soil, and plant ground cover if desired.

A loose-material border can also provide drainage (see page 36). Intersperse small boulders or tiles in the border for added beauty. To install tile edging, first pour a concrete footing; then set the tiles in mortar (see pages 96–97). Spanish roof tiles set on their sides (above) make a decorative statement and help hold loose materials in place.

Chapter Three

dry-laid patios and walks

A patio made of bricks or concrete pavers laid on a bed of firmly tamped gravel and sand is nearly as stable as a concrete slab. Flagstones set in soil are less secure, and may need to be readjusted from time to time. The projects in this chapter are definitely homeowner-friendly. No large weights need to be lifted, and no special skills are required. However, do work carefully, follow the steps in order, and avoid skipping ahead. Every so often, stand back and view your progress with a critical eye, so you can correct small mistakes before they become big problems.

A crushed limestone path meanders like a stream through grassy plants and boulders. The small stones are held in place with a casual edging made simply by setting medium-sized stones close to each other.

Flagstones of reddish sandstone run in two rough, parallel rows to form a path from the driveway to the house. Decorative plants poke through mulch laid between the stones.

Cobblestone-style concrete pavers have a rough surface and variegated coloring for a natural look, and are extremely durable.

White efflorescence often appears on natural bricks that are subject to moisture. On this walkway, what elsewhere might be considered an eyesore pleasingly complements moss growing in the joints.

Below: Relatively smooth, light gray flagstones contrast starkly with dark soil for a geometric look. If crevice plants are added the effect will be softened. These flagstones are set directly in the soil.

Rectangular-shaped flagstones in varied sizes wander through a bed of baby's tears, some of which fill the joints between the stones.

Birch logs laid side by side form a charming path, albeit one that must be tread on lightly. This decorative path is a simple solution for recycling a tree that had to be cut down.

A small section of blue and gray flagstones set in soil helps define this secluded seating area.

Below: *This pebble walkway is held in place by plastic edging that is completely hidden by plants spilling over onto the path.*

A surface made of
concrete pavers set in
a gravel-and-sand bed
is strong enough to
function as a driveway.

Tightly laid "semi-
dressed" stones—each
with at least one flat
side—form a distinctive
edging for a sand-laid
brick path.

These steps were made by first building frames out of landscaping timbers and 2x lumber, then filling the frames in with pebbles. Though casual in appearance, the stairway was laid out precisely, so all the steps are equal in length and height.

stepping-stones

Stepping-stones offer an easy way to create a decorative light-traffic path. Such a path is not practical for carrying garbage or groceries though, because the surface is uneven. For a flatter and more reliable path, install edging-enclosed pavers, duckboards, or compacted gravel (see pages 62–63, 68–69, or 74–75).

For the stepping-stones, choose flagstones that are roughly the same size and thickness, as shown on these pages.

Alternatively, buy pre-made concrete stepping-stones. Round pieces with an exposed aggregate surface are popular, as are square or octagonal concrete pavers that are about 12 inches in width.

ARRANGE THE STONES ON THE LAWN

There are two approaches to stepping-stone arrangement: The method shown here is to set out one stone per adult step. The other approach is to arrange flag-stones much as you would for a flagstone patio, with fairly consis-tent joints between the stones, in a 2- to 3-foot-wide pathway (see pages 56–57).

String mason's lines to arrange a basically straight path, or two hoses to help lay out a curved path. The strings or hoses should be about 2 feet apart. Place the stones on the lawn within the two lines or hoses, alternating from the left to the right edge, and have family members walk on them.

SETTING THE STONES

Stepping-stones can be simply set in tamped soil, but adding a bit of sand makes installation easier.

1 Mark a Stone's Outline
When setting manufactured concrete steppers, simply step or tap on a stone to create an impression in the grass in the shape of the paver. To mark the outline of a flagstone, use a shovel or trowel to slice a line through the sod all around the stone.

2 Cut Away Sod, Remove Soil
Use a shovel or a garden trowel to dig up and remove the sod under the stone. Dig deep enough so that after adding $\frac{1}{2}$ inch of sand the stone will be just below grade—low enough so you can run a lawn mower over it.

3 Add Sand, Replace Stone, Tap
Add about $\frac{1}{2}$ inch of damp sand to the hole, and spread it out, estimating the shape of the stone's underside. Set the stone in place. If it is too high for a lawn mower, dig the hole deeper. Once the stone is at the correct height, tap it with a rubber mallet or step on the stone.

4 Fill Voids and Replace Stone
Lift the stone to reveal the pattern of voids underneath. Fill the voids with sand, and replace the stone. Test the installation by walking on the stone. If it wobbles, pick it up and add sand where needed.

brick and paver patterns

To achieve a richly textured look on a patio surface, arrange modular pavers in a pattern, as shown on this page. Or use shaped "interlocking" pavers as shown on the opposite page.

PATTERNS USING RECTANGULAR UNITS

A jack-on-jack pattern requires the fewest cuts and is the simplest to install. But don't be afraid to try another pattern. As long as you have a wet-cutting masonry saw (see page 55), good attention to detail, and an extra half day or so, none of the patterns shown is diffi-

cult to install. The basketweave pattern, though exotic-looking, is actually one of the easiest to install.

For the pinwheel pattern, every fifth paver must be half-sized. In the running bond and herringbone patterns (shown below), every other paver along one side must be half-sized. If half-sized pavers are not available pre-cut, you can mass-produce them using a masonry saw.

The 45-degree herringbone pattern looks the most difficult, but a high-quality masonry saw will make quick work of all the 45-degree cuts.

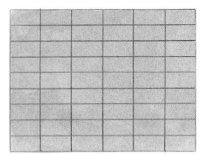

JACK-ON-JACK

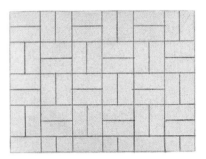

BASKETWEAVE

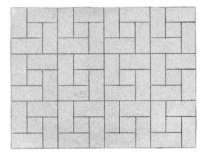

PINWHEEL

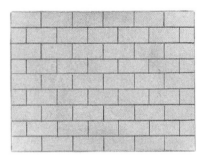

RUNNING BOND

45-DEGREE HERRINGBONE

INTERLOCKING PAVERS

It is often thought that interlocking pavers form a stronger surface than rectangular units. The truth is that any shape and pattern will be firm as long as all the pavers are tightly fitted together, and their joints are filled with fine sand. The real advantage of interlocking pavers is that they produce interesting patterns with little effort.

With some types of pavers, you need only one shape. Other interlocking pavers come in ensembles, so that you combine two or more shapes to produce the desired effect. Large pavers with stamped patterns install quickly, but they can be heavy.

Many concrete pavers come in variegated colors, which lends an overall rustic look. You may need to "shuffle" the pavers so you don't end up with pavers of only one color in a certain area. Some pavers have rough edges but still fit together easily.

cutting bricks, pavers, and flagstones

When building a brick wall, the cuts do not have to be precise, so bricklayers usually cut the bricks by hand. However, patio bricks usually need to be cut with precision, and concrete pavers are virtually impossible to cut by hand. Rent a masonry saw to do the job right.

CUTTING BY HAND

Professional bricklayers can cut bricks quickly by hacking at them with a brick trowel. This takes time to learn, so a homeowner is usually better off using a brickset chisel. Cutting by hand does not always work. Sometimes the brick cracks in an unexpected place. In that case, throw the pieces to one side and try again. Wear gloves and protective eyewear when cutting bricks, because chips will fly around.

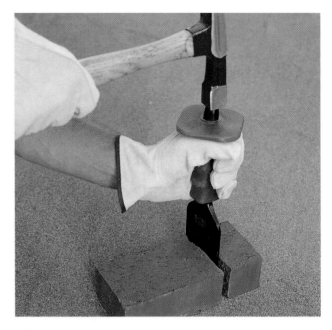

1 Score and Break
Place the brick on a flat, resilient surface, such as a bed of sand or a lawn. Position the tip of a brickset chisel on the brick, and tap with a hammer to score a line. Repeat on all four sides of the brick. Lay the brick flat, and hold the brickset against a score line, with its bevel (the angled side of the tip) facing the waste side of the cut. Give the brickset one hard whack to break the brick.

Cut a Flagstone

Cutting flagstone is even less predictable than cutting brick, so don't be surprised if you have to try several times before achieving the cut you want. Use a brickset or a narrow cold chisel to score a line on both sides of the flagstone. Position the stone with the scored line on top of a scrap piece of wood or a pipe. Using a hand sledge, hit the stone hard on the waste side to break it off.

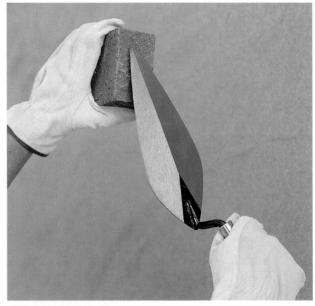

2 Clean the Cut Edge
Chip or scrape away any protrusions on the cut edge using the sharp side of a brick hammer or a brick trowel.

USING A WET-CUTTING MASONRY SAW

When you rent a wet-cutting masonry saw—also called a tub saw—specify the type of material you will be cutting, so the rental company can equip the saw with the correct blade. Be sure to obtain complete instructions for using the saw. Test the saw to make sure the tray glides smoothly and is square to the blade. If you need to make angle cuts, check that you have all the attachments you need.

Water must spray onto the blade at all times. If you cut for even a few seconds with a dry blade, you could burn out the blade. On some wet saws, the pump must be placed in a 5-gallon bucket filled with water; when the water runs out, it must be refilled by opening a drain hole in the pan of the saw and running the water back into the bucket. On other models, the pump is placed in the pan, so there is rarely a need to refill.

ANGLE CUT: Typical attachments hold the paver at a 45-, 60-, or 22½-degree angle to the blade. Hold the paver firmly against the attachment as you slide the paver forward to make the cut.

STRAIGHT CUT: Place the paver in the tray and hold it against the back guide so it is square to the blade. Turn on the saw, and check that water flows to the blade. Slide the tray forward slowly to slice through the paver.

CURVED CUT: Cutting a curve takes time and patience. Hold the paver firmly with both hands and tilt the front end of the paver up so the bottom of the cut will be slightly deeper than the top. Press the paver gently against the rotating blade and move it from side to side, removing only a small amount at a time.

Cutting with a Circular Saw
You can cut a few pavers using a circular saw equipped with a masonry cutting blade or a pricey diamond blade. Work slowly, and give the saw a rest if it starts to heat up. Wear a dust mask; cutting this way produces clouds of concrete or brick dust.

flagstones set in soil

Setting flagstones in soil is a quick and popular way to make a patio or walkway. The resulting surface will be rough and uneven, but smooth enough for most outdoor activities.

As much as possible, choose flagstones that have consistent thickness; if one stone is much thicker than adjacent stones, it will take additional time and effort to achieve an even surface. A stoneyard may allow you to hand-pick flagstones for a small patio, but for a surface larger than 100 square feet you will probably need to buy a pallet of stones. A salesperson can tell you how many tons of stone are needed to cover your square footage; this figure will vary dramatically depending on the thickness of the stones.

Have the stones delivered as close to the site as possible. Sort the stones in piles according to size—small, medium, and large. Choose stones from each pile as you lay the patio, so that stones of various sizes will be evenly distributed throughout the patio.

The step-by-step instructions show how to lay stones directly in soil. This is the easiest method. Typically, once you've removed the sod, the excavation is at the correct depth. Laying stones in soil also allows crevice plants to sink their roots deep into the ground with ease. To lay flagstones in a 2-inch-thick bed of sand, follow the steps for a paver patio (see pages 58–61). However, because flagstones are irregular, you will need to adjust the sand level for each stone.

1 Excavate, Tamp, and Rake
Remove sod and all roots from the patio area (see page 28). The excavation does not need to be flat, but it should generally slope away from the house if you expect a lot of rain. Dig deep enough so that the flagstones will be slightly below grade, allowing you to run a lawn mower over them. Tamp the soil with a hand tamper, then gently rake the area to loosen a layer of soil about ½ inch thick.

2 Set Stones in a Dry Run

Set stones in the excavated area and experiment with different arrangements until you achieve joints that are more or less consistent in width. Take your time. If a stone runs outside the excavated area, you may choose to dig away the sod rather than cutting the stone.

3 Cut Stones as Needed

See page 54 for cutting techniques. If a stone is very large, score lines and break it apart. The resulting pieces can be separated and will form neat joints.

4 Embed the Flagstones

Once you have arranged about 10 square feet of stones in a satisfactory pattern, embed them one at a time. Stand on a stone or tap it with a rubber mallet to produce an impression in the soil that shows the high and low spots. Pick the stone up on one end, and use a garden trowel to scrape and fill as needed. Lay the stone back down and stand on it. You'll probably need to pick it up and work the soil underneath one or two more times before the stone is free of wobbles and is level with its neighbors.

5 Fill Joints with Soil

Once all the stones are firmly bedded, use a pointed shovel or a garden trowel to fill the joints with soil. Allow the soil to dry; then gently brush soil off the stones.

6 Spray and Refill

Adjust a hose nozzle to produce a fine mist, and spray the patio until the soil in the joints is thoroughly wet. This will compact the soil, causing it to sink. Wait for the soil to dry, then add more, and spray again. Repeat until the soil in the joints is at the desired height. If you choose, sprinkle seeds of your choice onto the joints, or brush with a moss mixture (see page 78).

laying a paver patio

Once the site has been laid out, excavated, edged, and filled with well-tamped compactible gravel (see pages 26–39), you are ready to add landscaping fabric, any temporary screed guides, sand, and the pavers. These pages show laying paving bricks; follow the same steps to install concrete pavers.

Arrange to have the sand and bricks delivered close to the site. If possible, have the coarse underlayment sand dumped on top of the landscaping fabric. Buy fine sand (see step 12) in large bags. The pavers will probably come in large, very heavy pallets, so choose a spot where they will not damage your lawn.

1 Spread Landscaping Fabric
Roll landscaping or plastic sheeting over the gravel base. Cut the pieces carefully, and butt them tightly against the edging; that is where weeds are most likely to grow. Overlap the strips by 6 to 8 inches. Hold the sheeting in place with small mounds of sand to keep it from blowing away.

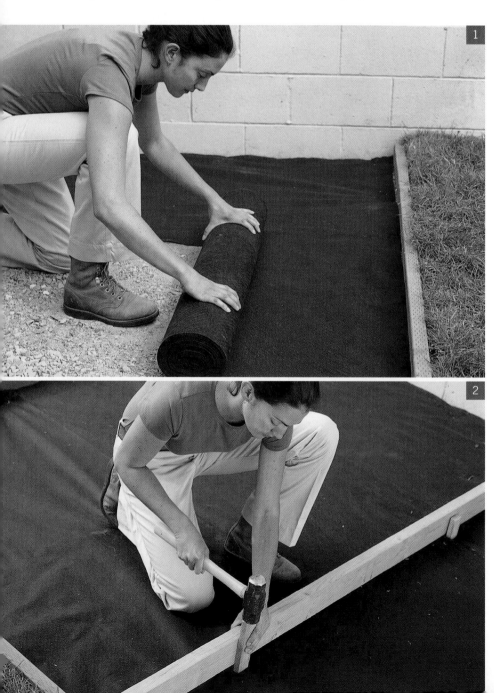

2 Install a Temporary Screed Guide
If your patio is less than 8 feet wide, skip this step. For a larger patio, cut a 2 × 4 to fit, and attach it 6 to 10 feet away from the edging so that its top is exactly at the same height as the edging. Screw or nail it to the edging or to the house at either end. Every 3 or 4 feet, drive a 2 × 4 stake on the outside of the area to be screeded (see step 5), about an inch below the top of the 2 × 4. Check the temporary screed to see if it's either level or correctly sloped.

3 Make a Screed

Start with a straight piece of 2 × 4 or 2 × 6 that is about 2 feet longer than the area to be screeded. Cut one or more strips of plywood to the thickness of the pavers, plus the width of the 2 × 4 or 2 × 6. The plywood should be about 4 inches shorter than the area to be screeded. Attach the plywood with screws as shown.

4 Spread Sand

Taking care not to damage the landscaping fabric, spread the sand with a square shovel and a rake until it is slightly higher than it needs to be (see step 5). The sand should be a little damp; if at any point it dries out, spray it with a hose nozzle set on mist.

5 Screed the Sand

If the screed guide is longer than 7 feet, do this step with a helper. Starting at one end, move the screed across the patio to smooth the sand to the depth of a paver thickness. It may help to saw back and forth as you move the screed along. Fill in any voids and repeat until you achieve a perfectly smooth surface.

6 Stretch a Guide Line

Temporarily stretch a mason's line across the area to act as a height guide. Attach it to wood edging with a nail or screw. If you have paver edging, use a spare paver as a weight as shown.

7 Lay the First Pavers

Start in one corner, and set several bricks to abut the edging. Use a level or straightedge to check that the pavers are at the desired height; if they are not, adjust the screed, and screed again. Aim to set the pavers straight down onto the bed; if you slide a paver more than ¼ inch or so, you will create waves in the sand and the surface will not be level. Install the pavers so they touch each other.

8 Tap with a Beater Board to Align the Tops

After 10 or 12 pavers have been set, place a beater board—a straight 2 × 4 or 2 × 6 about 24 inches long—on top and tap it with a hammer or mallet. If a paver is noticeably higher than its neighbor, tap it down.

9 Continue Laying Pavers

As you continue laying pavers, move the string guide every 2 feet or so. If at some point you need to kneel on top of the patio, lay down a piece of plywood large enough to support your toes as well as your knees to protect the screeded sand.

10 Screed the Other Side of a Temporary Screed Guide

If you installed a temporary screed guide, remove it once you have finished with one section. Then spread sand in the next section. Rest the screed on the patio surface at one end and the edging on the other side, screed the sand, and lay pavers.

11 Move Edging to Minimize Cutting

You may be able to avoid cutting pavers at one edge of the patio by adjusting the edging. Install pavers to the end of the patio; then move the edging to abut them. In the case of 2× edging, have a helper push the edging up against the pavers while you drive screws and stakes to secure it. You will have to cut the corner using a handsaw or reciprocating saw.

12 Sweep Fine Sand into the Joints

Scatter very fine sand over the pavers, and use a soft bristled broom to sweep the sand into the joints. If the sand is wet, allow it to dry and sweep again.

13 Run a Vibrating Plate Compactor over the Surface

This will cause the fine sand to settle down into the joints. Sweep more sand into the joints and tamp again; repeat until the joints stay full.

The Dry Mortar Method

If you live in a warm area where it rarely freezes, here's an alternate technique: Excavate, install edging, lay and power-tamp a gravel bed, and screed a layer of sand as you would for a standard dry-laid patio. Use plastic tile spacers to lay the pavers with ⅜- to ½-inch joints between them. Combine a bag of dry mortar mix with two shovels of Portland cement; keep the mix completely dry as you work. Shovel the mix onto the surface and sweep it into the cracks. Remove the plastic spacers and sweep again. Sweep carefully so the pavers are clean and consistent in depth. Spray the surface with the nozzle set on "mist"; thoroughly soak the joints, but avoid making puddles. Tool the joints as you would a brick wall (see page 115). As soon as the mortar hardens, scrub the surface with the water and a brush. A day later, clean away any haze or mortar splotches by brushing with a weak solution of muriatic acid.

laying pavers with wide joints

If you want a patio with a soft, comfortable look, consider installing large paving units, such as adobe, flagstones, or concrete stepping pavers, spaced so that the joints are ¾ inch to 1½ inches wide. Bricks and other small pavers can be installed with joints ½ to ¾ inches wide; installing them farther apart will probably look sloppy.

The resulting surface will not be as firm as a tight-laid patio; you may need to reset a wobbly paver or two every couple of years. Crevice plants will be a major part of the final look of this type of patio.

Mixed Material Patios

Just about any material that can survive your climate can be incorporated into a patio or path. It may look sloppy if materials butt tightly against each other, but plants growing in wide joints can make it charming. Here, flagstones and river rocks create a whimsical courtyard patio.

Although you can use any edging, large paving units usually look best with either massive landscaping timbers or nearly invisible plastic or steel edging.

EXCAVATING AND INSTALLING EDGING

To avoid cutting the last row, lay the blocks in a dry run, with 1-inch joints between, to decide the size of the patio. The joint sizes can be made ¼ inch larger or smaller in order to suit your particular situation.

Lay out for the patio, remove the sod, and install the edging of your choice (see pages 26–35). Excavate, taking into account the full thickness of the blocks. Spread gravel and tamp using a vibrating plate compactor (see pages 38–39). Add landscaping fabric if it is recommended in your area. Add 1 to 2 inches of sand, and screed (see pages 58–59).

SETTING BLOCKS IN A GRID

Lightly mark the edging pieces for the positions of the blocks; make a mark in the center of each joint line. Using the marks, stretch mason's lines to mark out a section that will encompass a certain number of blocks (9 is a common number). Position the blocks inside the section; then stand back to check that the joints are relatively consistent.

If you need to move blocks, don't slide them. Pick them up and set them down, to avoid disturbing the sand underneath. Use a level or a straight board to check that the blocks are even with each other. If necessary, tap a block with a rubber mallet,

or pick it up and add sand underneath it.

Once one section is complete, move the string lines and proceed to the next. Never kneel directly on the sand; kneel on a piece of plywood that is long enough to accommodate your toes as well.

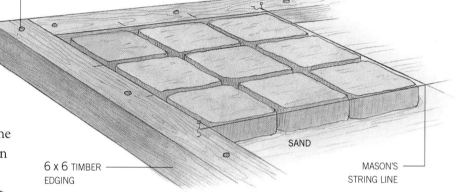

REBAR ANCHOR

6 x 6 TIMBER EDGING

SAND

MASON'S STRING LINE

FILLING THE JOINTS

Using a square-bladed shovel, fill the joints with soil or sand. Either sweep as you go, or wait for the sand or soil to dry before sweeping.

Gently tamp the joints using a piece of 1 × lumber. Then fill and sweep them again. Spray with a fine mist, allow it to dry, and fill in any voids. Plant seed in the joints if you wish.

installing wood blocks and rounds

Wood can be a surprisingly long-lived paving material, provided you choose the lumber carefully and install it correctly. Wood rounds and blocks are often installed with the grain facing up. That orientation means the wood will soak in moisture readily, but it also allows wood to dry out quickly.

CHOOSING MATERIALS

Choose wood that has proved durable in your area. Pressure-treated lumber rated "ground contact" is the most reliable, and can last for decades as long as it can dry out after rainfalls. The dark heartwood of redwood, cedar, or cypress will not last as long. To prolong the life of blocks or rounds, soak them in a sealer/preservative that contains an insecticide; consult with a local lumberyard to see what works in your area.

Wood rounds are not available at most lumberyards. However, you may find cedar or cypress poles—essentially, straight branches with the bark trimmed off. The lumberyard may cut these into 3-inch-long rounds for a modest price.

If a neighbor is cutting down a tree, it can be sliced into rounds using a chain saw. Using a chain saw can be dangerous, so approach this job with caution. The resulting rounds most likely will be quite irregular in thickness, making them difficult but certainly not

impossible to install. You may choose to leave the bark on the rounds, but be aware that it may come apart and rot in a year or so.

CUTTING TIMBERS INTO BLOCKS

If you have plenty of time, or if you need only a few blocks, it's not difficult to cut 4 × 4s and 4 × 6s using a standard 7¼-inch circular saw. To cut lots of blocks, use a power miter saw (also called a chopsaw) or a radial-arm saw. A 10-inch saw will cut 4 × 4s, but you will need a 12-inch saw to cut through 6 × 6s or 4 × 6s.

Set up a simple jig like the one shown at right. Anchor the saw firmly, perhaps to a 2 × 12 resting on stable sawhorses. Place blocks on the 2 × 12 at the same height as the base of the saw, so you can easily rest a timber in place and slide it over after each cut. Anchor a stop block 3 inches or so from the blade, so that each cut block will be exactly the same length.

The jig will allow you to cut factory style, but avoid working too quickly or you may burn out the blade—or even worse, the saw. Give your equipment a rest when the saw starts to feel hot. If the cutting starts to go slowly, you probably need a new blade.

SETTING BLOCKS OR ROUNDS

Install wood blocks for the most part as you would a paver patio, establishing a gravel and sand base and enclosing them with a strong edging. However, do not power tamp the blocks once they are in place. Sweep sand into the joints only once; small gaps in the joint lines are actually desired, since they give the wood extra breathing space.

Wood rounds will probably not be consistent in depth, and they are certainly not uniform in shape. After setting up the gravel and sand base, experiment with different arrangements until you obtain a pleasing pattern. You will have to dig away or add sand under each round, much as for flagstone (see page 57). Use a straightedge to check that the rounds are at the same height. Fill the gaps between the rounds with gravel or large pebbles for good drainage.

fabricating duckboards

Modular decking sections, often called duckboards, can be arranged and rearranged to suit your needs. Scatter them on a lawn to create an informal path, or lay them close together to form a low-lying deck.

Use rot-resistant lumber, especially for the sleepers (the underlying framing members). You may choose pressure-treated lumber for the sleepers and cedar or redwood for the decking boards, for example.

See the sidebar on page 69 for size and measurement information before starting your project.

1 Build a Jig
Cut four 2 × 4s to the desired length of the decking boards plus about 10 inches. Position them in a square pattern as shown. See that the distance between the boards in each direction is the same as the desired length of the decking boards, and check all the corners for square. Drill a pilot hole and drive two 2½-inch screws into each joint. Check again for square.

2 Cut the Decking Boards
Set up a power saw with a jig, so you can cut all the boards to the same length. Each duckboard in this design uses six 2 × 4 decking boards and two 2 × 3 sleepers.

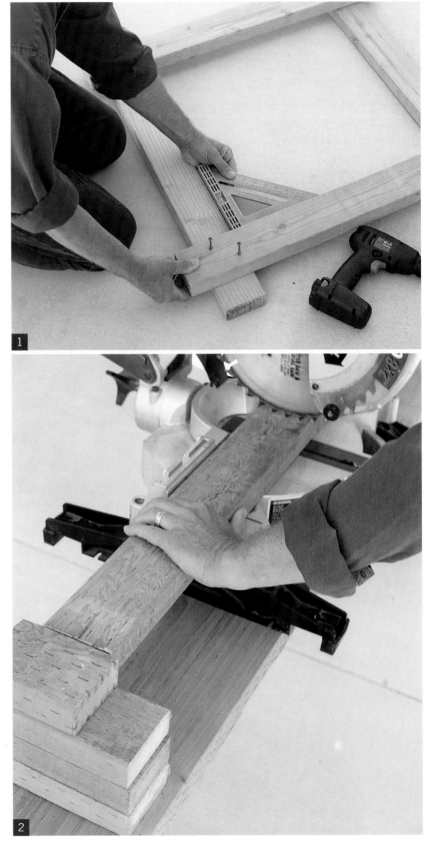

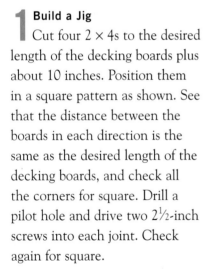

3

4

3 Assemble with Screws
Set the sleepers at either end, and place the decking boards on top. Use nails as spacers to maintain consistent joints between the decking boards. Drill pilot holes and drive two 2½-inch deck screws into each joint.

4 Lay the Duckboards in Place
Ideally, duckboards should be placed on a flat area that has been excavated and filled with non-compactible gravel or pebbles for good drainage. You can lay duckboards on a concrete slab, but be sure to position them so rainwater can easily drain underneath; all the sleepers should be parallel to the flow of water.

In a heavy traffic area, you may choose to screw the duckboards together. Drill pilot holes and drive 2½-inch deck screws to anchor two sleepers to each other.

Getting the Size Right
If a duckboard is to be square, the decking boards must be cut to a length that equals the width of a certain number of boards, including ⅛-inch joints. In our example, we cut 2 x 4s to 21⅝ inches—the width of six 2 x 4s (6 times 3½ inches, or 21 inches) plus five joints (5 times ⅛ inch, or ⅝ inch). Two other possible arrangements are nine 2 x 4s at 32½ inches, or five 2 x 6s (which are 5½ inches wide) at 28 inches. Of course, if you choose joints wider than ⅛ inch, the dimensions will change accordingly. Boards spanning more than 24 inches may be springy.

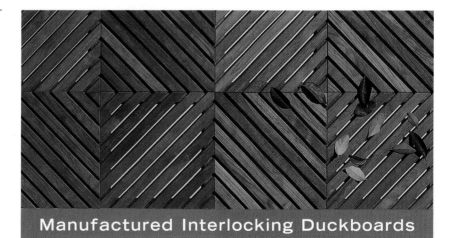

Manufactured Interlocking Duckboards

Ready-made duckboards like these are fairly pricey but are made of durable materials and fit together easily. These units are made of teak, which will turn a silvery gray unless stained regularly. The units join together with stainless-steel clips.

building steps

In a rustic setting that needs only two or three steps, construction can be casual. However, for a stairway to be comfortable to walk on, all the steps must have the same rise (the height of the step) and run (the length of the step). Inconsistent rises or runs will make a stairway a tripping hazard.

Steps should be at least 2 feet wide. Make them 4 to 5 feet wide if you want two people to walk abreast. Wide stairways also make comfortable places to sit and chat.

Wood and concrete steps are usually built with treads that are level. Outdoor steps made with timbers or masonry materials should have treads that are sloped at a rate of $\frac{1}{8}$ to $\frac{1}{4}$ inch per foot, so rainwater can easily flow down the stairs.

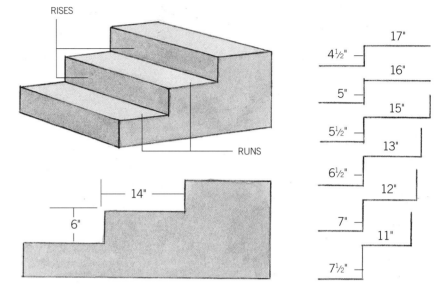

CALCULATING RISE AND RUN

A rise should be between 5 and 8 inches. To be comfortable and safe, a stairway needs a proper balance of rise and run. The rule is that the horizontal run for each step plus twice the vertical rise should equal 25 to 27 inches. For instance, if the rise is $5\frac{1}{2}$ inches (the thickness of a 6×6), the tread should be around 15 inches ($5\frac{1}{2}$ times 2 is 11; 11 plus 15 is 26). If the rise is greater, then the run must become smaller: a step with a $7\frac{1}{2}$-inch rise requires a run that is around 11 inches.

To calculate the rise and run on a sloped area, hold a long, straight board with a level on top and measure down from it to find the stairway's total rise. Divide the total rise by the desired rise height for each step to find out how many steps you need. Then multiply the number of steps by the run for each step to estimate the total length of the stairway.

You may need to adjust the rise or run, or even the number of steps, to make it all come out right. Make a drawing on a piece of paper to help you envision the stairway. Make sure the bottom and top steps will be the same height as all the others.

LOG AND SOIL STEPS

Log and soil steps are easy to build, and are especially suitable for occasional steps on a site that slopes too gently to qualify for standard steps. You can use logs, as shown at right, or 6×6 landscaping timbers. Essentially, each log or timber acts as a small retaining wall.

Steps like these may slope as much as $1\frac{1}{2}$ inch per foot. Lay out the steps using mason's lines and stakes. In some cases, you may need to cut into the side of the hill with a square shovel to make a trench for the logs. Alternatively, you can install the logs on top of the ground and then fill in behind with soil. Anchor each log or timber by drilling holes and driving reinforcing bars; see page 73. Once the steps are made, fill in with soil and plant grass or add wood chips.

TIMBER AND GRAVEL STEPS

More serious steps like those shown at left should follow the layout guidelines on the opposite page. Excavate and lay the timbers as shown on pages 72–73; then simply fill in with the gravel of your choice. The treads on these steps can be level, since water will easily soak down through the gravel.

putting in a loose-material path

The easiest path or patio surface to install is one made of loose materials, but don't take the task lightly. The area must be excavated in the same way as for a paver path or patio. The edging must be installed firmly or the gravel will stray outside the path. This will cause trouble when you mow the lawn.

How "loose" will the final surface be? That depends on the material. Pebbles and large-size gravel will be easily kicked aside; bicycles and wheelbarrows will have trouble rolling and will make dents. Other materials, such as crushed rock or small-grained decomposed granite, can form a surface that is nearly as hard as asphalt once it is compacted. Ask your supplier how various materials perform in your area.

Setting Stepping-Stones Amid Loose Materials

This arrangement combines the look of loose materials with a fairly stable path. Excavate, install edging, and spread and tamp gravel as for a patio. For each stepping-stone, shovel an inch or so of sand on top of the gravel, and work to make the stone stable. Once all the stones are installed, spread and rake the loose material to fill between them, taking care not to dislodge the stones.

1 Spread and Spray the Gravel Base

Excavate to a depth of 3 or 4 inches, install the edging, and tamp the ground firm (see pages 28–39). If it is recommended in your area, cover the soil with a layer of landscaping fabric. Shovel and rake a 1½-inch layer of compactible gravel, taking care not to disturb the fabric. Spray the gravel with a fine mist to wet it thoroughly without forming puddles.

2 Compress the Base

You can use a vibrating plate compactor (see page 39) to compress the base, but a drum roller may be easier to navigate on a narrow path. The base must be firmly compressed, or less attractive stones may work their way up through the finished surface.

Turf Block

3 Spread and Rake the Top Coat

Dump the finish material into the path, taking care not to disturb the base coat. Spread it with a garden rake. If the material is small-grained, you can tamp it with a vibrating plate compactor or a drum roller. Do not attempt to tamp large pebbles or stones.

Turf block, a product made of concrete cast in ornamental shapes, is making a modest comeback. Properly installed, it provides a surface strong enough to be used as a driveway while allowing grass to grow through.

Lay the block in a gravel-and-sand bed, as you would a paver patio. Fill the cells of the turf block with soil about ½ inch below the top of the turf block, and plant grass seed in the soil.

demolishing and reusing an old concrete slab

If you have a concrete slab—a sidewalk, driveway, or patio—that needs a face-lift, first identify the problem and ponder the possible remedies:

- If you simply do not like the look of concrete even though it is in good shape, consider applying a stain, or engraving it; see the solutions on pages 92–93.
- If the concrete is stained, try cleaning it with a concrete cleaning product.
- If one section of concrete is free of serious cracks but has sunk below its neighbor, call concrete contractors to see if they can raise it up using a technique called mud jacking.
- If there is a pattern of thin hairline cracks all over the surface of a slab, the problem will only get worse over time if left untreated. Apply sealer to keep the cracking in check. You can also resurface; see page 94.
- If one side of a crack is higher than the other side, then the crack runs all the way through the slab. If you have only one or two of these cracks, you can fill them with concrete patch. If there are numerous cracks of this type, the slab should be removed.

REMOVING OLD CONCRETE

Usually, a concrete slab is not nearly as difficult to demolish as you may think. Most residential sidewalks and patios are only 2 to 3 inches thick. Driveways are usually thicker, and often are reinforced with a wire mesh. If a slab has a number of serious cracks, it's probably not very thick.

Once you've determined that a slab must go, there's little harm in trying to break it up yourself. If the task proves too hard, you can call in pros. You may want to start breaking concrete in an out-of-the-way corner, to gauge the difficulty.

1 Break Up the Concrete
Wear long sleeves and pants, gloves, a dust mask, and eye protection. If the concrete is in very bad shape, simply whack it with a sledge hammer, and it may break apart. Usually, however, the concrete is resting firmly on the ground. Insert a wrecking bar, which is about 6 feet long, under the slab. You may have to dig with a shovel to create an insertion point for the bar. Place a stone or scrap of lumber under the bar to act as a fulcrum, and pry up the concrete. Have a helper hold the concrete up while you beat the concrete with a sledge hammer; it will probably break apart with relative ease.

2 Haul It Away

If wire reinforcing mesh is embedded in the concrete, cut it with bolt cutters or side-cutting pliers. Break the concrete into manageable chunks—there's no sense risking injury trying to lift heavy pieces. Haul away the concrete to a dump site approved for concrete, or reuse the concrete.

REUSING CONCRETE CHUNKS

Once it is broken up, concrete can make a surprisingly useful landscaping material—and you certainly can't argue with the price. To shape the chunks for your purposes, simply hit the edges with a small sledge hammer. Be sure to wear protective clothing when you do this.

The broken edge of a concrete chunk—the part that will be most visible when the chunk is used as a wall material—reveals a surprisingly attractive pattern of cement and rocks of various sizes. The chunks will be fairly consistent in thickness, making them easy

to stack for a simple dry wall; follow the techniques on pages 120–121.

Older concrete may have a worn surface that displays small stones. Lay pieces like these in soil or sand for a patio. Make the joints wide and fill them with showy crevice plants or moss.

choosing crevice plants

Small plants that grow in joints soften the appearance of a patio or wall. Check planting instructions before you fill joints with soil. Some plants require a good potting soil, while others do fine in sandy dirt. Choose plants with watering requirements similar to those of surrounding plants. Thyme, for example, requires little moisture and is easily overwatered.

Larger crevice plants are best for light-traffic areas; use smaller plants if you expect them to be walked on often. A spreading or creeping plant adds more greenery but may be trampled; some quick-growing types may grab too much territory.

To quickly propagate moss, dissolve a fist-size lump of porcelain clay (available at a crafts or art supply store) in 3 cups of water and stir until the mixture has the consistency of a thick milkshake. Add 1 cup of undiluted liquid fish fertilizer and 1 cup of moss. Thoroughly whip with a wire whisk, and paint or slather the mixture where you want it to grow.

Shown clockwise from top: ice plant, oregano, sedum 'Vera Jameson', and aubrieta grow in a dry stone wall; purple verbena; bellflower; white sweet alyssum, blue star creeper, and carex; Scotch moss.

Chapter Four

working with concrete

Concrete is the workhorse of outdoor building materials. A properly laid concrete slab will last for generations; a concrete footing, if it is sufficiently massive, will support a wall and hold it steady for just as long. Think of concrete as a blank canvas. A plain slab can be covered with tile, brick, or stone. A concrete (or concrete block) wall can be faced with stone or covered with stucco and painted. A new generation of concrete paints and stains can make existing concrete beautiful. And various techniques are available to enliven the look of concrete as you pour it.

figuring concrete needs

In many areas, you need a building permit before pouring concrete; check with your local building department. Be sure to follow the inspector's instructions to the letter.

CONCRETE INGREDIENTS AND ADDITIVES

Basic concrete is composed of Portland cement, sand, gravel (also called aggregate), and water.

Portland cement is the glue that holds it all together. The more cement, the stronger the concrete will be. If you are mixing a small amount of concrete or mortar and want to strengthen it, simply add a shovel or two of cement. When ordering from a ready-mixed concrete company, specify how much cement you want: A "six-bag mix" contains six bags of cement per yard of concrete, making it strong enough for most projects.

Gravel stones should be no larger than one third the thickness of the slab; usually stones are ¾ inch or smaller. There should be enough sand to fill in the spaces between the gravel stones.

If dirt gets into a concrete mix, the concrete will be weakened.

An inspector may test wet concrete for "slump" by setting a 12-inch cone of concrete on the ground and seeing how much it sags. If it sags 4 or 5 inches, it is about the right consistency—not too soupy and not too dry—for most jobs.

If you live in an area with freezing winters, consider ordering air-entrained concrete, which contains tiny air bubbles. The bubbles lend the concrete a bit of flexibility, so it is less likely to crack in cold weather. Air-entrained concrete is available only from a concrete truck.

If freezing weather is possible on the day of the pour, consider ordering an accelerating additive, which makes the concrete harden quicker. If the weather is hot and dry, consider adding a retardant, which slows up the drying time. If the concrete sets too fast, you may not have enough time to adequately finish the surface.

CALCULATING CONCRETE NEEDS

You can use the following guidelines to figure gravel and sand needs as well as concrete. Begin by taking careful measurements of the area to be filled. Measure for thickness in a number of spots to obtain a reliable average; a discrepancy of ½ inch can make a big difference in the amount of concrete you need.

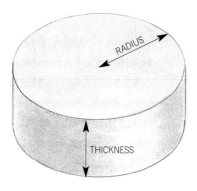

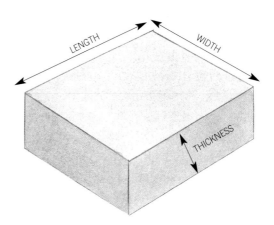

When ordering concrete, tell the supplier the dimensions—the square footage and depth. A supplier can quickly calculate how much you need. However, it is a good idea for you to double-check the calculations as well.

Concrete is usually sold by the cubic yard, also just called a yard. A yard of concrete (or sand or gravel) fills an area 3 feet by 3 feet by 3 feet. For small projects like post holes, you may choose to measure cubic footage instead; bags of dry-mix concrete often have cubic footage printed on them.

Using a calculator, it's easy to figure out concrete needs. For a rectangular slab or footing, multiply the width in feet times the length in feet, times the thickness in inches. Divide the result by 12 to get the number of cubic feet. Divide that number by 27 to get the number of cubic yards. For example, if a slab measures 20 feet by 30 feet and is 3½ inches thick:

$20 \times 30 \times 3.5 = 2,100$
$2,100 \div 12 = 175$ cubic feet
$175 \div 27 = 6.48$ yards

Add about 10 percent for potential waste, and order a little more than 7 yards.

To figure concrete needs for a circular patio (which is actually a cylindrical shape), multiply the radius in feet squared times pi (3.14), times the thickness in inches. Divide that number by 12 to get the cubic feet. Divide that number by 27 to get the number of cubic yards. For example, if an area is 12 feet in radius and 4 inches thick:

$12 \times 12 = 144$
$144 \times 3.14 \times 4 = 1,808$
$1,808 \div 12 = 151$ cubic feet
$151 \div 27 = 5.6$ cubic yards

Add about 10 percent for potential waste, and order a little more than 6 yards.

MIX YOUR OWN OR HAVE IT DELIVERED?

If you need more than ¼ yard of concrete, ordering ready-mixed concrete is usually worth the extra expense. A 60-pound sack of dry-mix concrete makes about ½ cubic foot, meaning that you would need to mix 52 bags to make a yard of concrete.

Many ready-mixed concrete companies do not want to deliver less than a yard of concrete. Others have special trucks designed to

mix smaller amounts at the job site. If one company does not want your business, keep calling around.

If you live in a remote area or if you want to mix concrete in small batches, it might make sense to rent an electric-powered concrete mixer. You will need to mix Portland cement, sand, and gravel along with water; check with local builders or an inspector to make sure you buy the right proportions of the correct ingredients. Transporting the ingredients requires a pickup truck with a bed that seals tightly.

REINFORCING STEEL

To ensure against cracking, embed wire mesh in a slab, or reinforcing bar (rebar) in a footing. Steel reinforcement should be inserted into the middle of a slab or footing. Check with your building department or a local contractor to find out the type of reinforcement needed in your area.

1 Lay Steel Reinforcement

To flatten a roll of reinforcing mesh, first unroll it; then roll it backwards. Cut it to fit between the forms using wire cutters, and lay it in place. Every 2 feet or so, use a metal bolster to raise the mesh above the base. Check that the mesh is below the level of the forms.

2 Install Isolation Joints

Where the slab will abut the house, snap a chalk line to indicate the height of the slab. Using construction adhesive, glue a strip of fibrous isolation joint to the house.

3 Load the Wheelbarrow

Set a wheelbarrow on a stable surface under the truck's chute. If you are not experienced, ask the driver to load the wheelbarrow only half full. You can increase the loads once you get used to the work. Use a scrap of lumber to scrape the chute after it stops pouring, so no concrete spills onto the ground.

4 Pour into the Formed Area

Wheel the concrete to a far corner of the formed area. Pour the concrete out. Have a helper spread the concrete with a shovel so that it comes up to the correct height. Note: If you start to lose control of the wheelbarrow, don't try to right it. Instead, push down on the handles with both hands. Then pick up the handles and start again.

5 Screed the Concrete

Working with a helper, position a long, straight 2 × 4 screed so the ends rest on forms, or on a form and a temporary screed guide. Using a sawing back-and-forth motion, draw the screed across the surface to flatten the concrete roughly at the desired height. If there are voids (low spots), fill them by shoveling in concrete, and screed again.

6 Move a Temporary Screed Guide

If the slab is large enough to need a temporary screed guide, fill and screed the other section as you did the first; then remove the guide. Pour a shovel or two of concrete into the resulting trough.

decorative effects for new concrete driveways and patios

Concrete need not be plain gray. A number of techniques allow you to change its texture and color. Approach this task cautiously, however. Pouring a slab (see pages 80–87) is enough of a challenging task; adding another step may be more than you can handle. Most of these techniques can be learned in an hour or two, but you won't have that much time to spare when you pour the concrete. Pour a small section of concrete and practice the technique until you are adept at it. Or hire a pro.

Decorative concrete is a booming business in many parts of the country. Local contractors may offer customers a wide range of special effects and colors.

These two pages show how to create special effects in concrete while it is being poured. See pages 92–95 for ways to dress up or repair existing concrete.

SEEDED AGGREGATE

One popular approach uses seed aggregate—attractive pebbles or stones. Have bags of the aggregate on hand. Pour and float the slab, edge the joints, and make control joints. As soon as the bleed water has evaporated, use a shovel to scatter the aggregate over the concrete. Cover the entire surface, but try to apply only one layer of aggregate. Use a wood or magnesium float (below) to press the aggregate down until the stones lie just below the surface. Refloat the concrete so that the aggregate is barely covered with a thin layer of cement.

When the slab starts to harden in about 30 to 60 minutes, have a helper spray the surface with a fine mist of water while you gently sweep with a broom to expose the aggregate. If the cement runs, stop sweeping and allow more time for it to dry. If you need to scrub aggressively, the concrete is starting to set, so work quickly to finish the job. Stop brushing once the tops of the stones show; if you expose too much of the stones, they could come loose later. Any cement haze left on the stones can be removed later with a 10 percent muriatic acid solution.

COLORING CONCRETE

As concrete is being poured, there are two ways to color it. For either one, buy dry concrete colorant. Check the label to see how much you need.

The most reliable (and most expensive) method is to mix the colorant with the dry concrete ingredients before you add water. This works best if you use white Portland cement instead of the standard gray. Usually, you can do this only if you plan to mix the concrete yourself. You may be able to find concrete delivery companies that offer colored concrete.

The second method is to dust the color on. Pour and roughly float the concrete with a darby or bull float. Sifting the colorant through your fingers as you scatter it, spread two-thirds of the recommended amount of colorant over the surface. Float the surface with a magnesium or wood float (above). Apply the remaining colorant, float again, and finish with a steel trowel or broom.

TRAVERTINE FINISH

A travertine finish produces a stucco-like texture. It should be used only in areas that do not have freezing winters. Roughly float the surface with a darby or bull float. In a bucket, mix one part wet cement with two parts sand; periodically remix as you work to maintain a consistent texture. You may want to add concrete colorant to the mix. Dip a large wallpaper or masonry brush into the mixture; then dash it onto the concrete surface, aiming for a consistent pattern of uneven scatterings.

When the slab is firm enough to support you on a knee board, gently run a straight trowel over the surface to knock down the high spots. The result is a stone-like texture, smooth on the high spots and rougher in the low spots.

STAMPING OR TOOLING

Stamping or tooling the concrete sounds easier than it is, and is best left to the pros. Using a stamping tool or a masonry jointer, make a pattern of indentations in the concrete surface to imitate the look of bricks or flagstones (as shown in the photo below). Once the bleed water evaporates, carefully float and finish the surface. You will need to retool some joints.

jazzing up existing concrete

Concrete that is structurally unsound should be removed and replaced (see pages 76–77). If a slab is strong but ugly, you have a number of options for adding appeal. In addition to the techniques shown on these pages, consider covering the concrete with tile or pavers (see pages 96–98).

Local concrete contractors may specialize in beautifying old slabs. Check out their displays, or visit slabs in your area that they have refinished.

Concrete that has become an eyesore may improve greatly if you clean it. Use a commercial product to soak up any surface oil and grease; then scrub the surface with a concrete cleaner. Using a pressure washer may also be effective. As a final resort, put on long clothes and rubber gloves, and apply a 10 percent solution of muriatic acid.

STAINING

Stain differs from paint because it penetrates the concrete rather than simply forming a film on top. Some manufacturers carry a special cleaner, containing acid, which must be applied first, so the concrete will be porous enough to soak up the stain. You may choose to stain the concrete with a single color. Or create decorative effects in much the same way as you would apply a faux finish to a wall. Paint a solid base color; then spatter blotches of another color using a large brush, a sponge, or even a paint sprayer. Professionals who specialize in staining concrete can make concrete look like large slabs of travertine or marble.

Two slabs of stained concrete surround a narrow strip filled with pebbles, for a driveway that is practical as well as beautiful.

An aging driveway was coated with a ½-inch-thick layer of polymer-enhanced concrete, then stamped and stained to create a random pattern.

Artistically applied, concrete stain can aptly complement natural brick.

CUT PATTERNS AND ENGRAVING

Using a concrete saw and a straightedge, you can cut a series of lines, about ⅛ inch deep, to divide a slab into sections. Use this technique to delineate large, regularly shaped areas, or create a pleasantly random pattern like the one that was stamped in the photo above. Once the lines are cut, the sections can be stained or painted in contrasting colors.

Some companies specialize in engraving concrete. They use special tools to create a pattern of shallow, meandering grooves that look like grout lines (as shown at left). The engraving is usually done after the concrete has been stained.

resurfacing concrete

Some products are designed to be sprayed, painted, or troweled onto an existing concrete surface, creating a new finish that is as thin as ¼ inch. These products tend to be fairly expensive, but may be worth the cost because of their ease of installation. If you need to cover only tiny hairline cracks or unsightliness, consider masonry paint, which may need to be reapplied yearly in high-traffic areas. Check with a local dealer to see which products have proved durable in your area.

TOP-COATING A SLAB

Shown below is a more tried-and-true method: applying a top coat that is 1 to 2 inches thick. If the concrete slab is firm and stable, 1 inch is thick enough. If not, adding 2 inches will help strengthen a weak slab.

Dig a small trench around the perimeter of the slab. Cut and place 2 × 4s up against the concrete, 1 to 2 inches above the surface of the concrete.

Drive stakes every 3 feet or so, and anchor them to the 2 × 4s with screws. Brush or roll a coat of latex concrete bonding agent onto the concrete.

Empty a bag of sand-mix concrete into a wheelbarrow, and then add a shovel or two of Portland cement. Mix in water to produce very stiff concrete—you will have to shovel the mixture rather than pour it. Apply the top coat onto the old concrete. Float and finish the coat as you would a standard slab, and cover with plastic so it cures slowly (see pages 86–87).

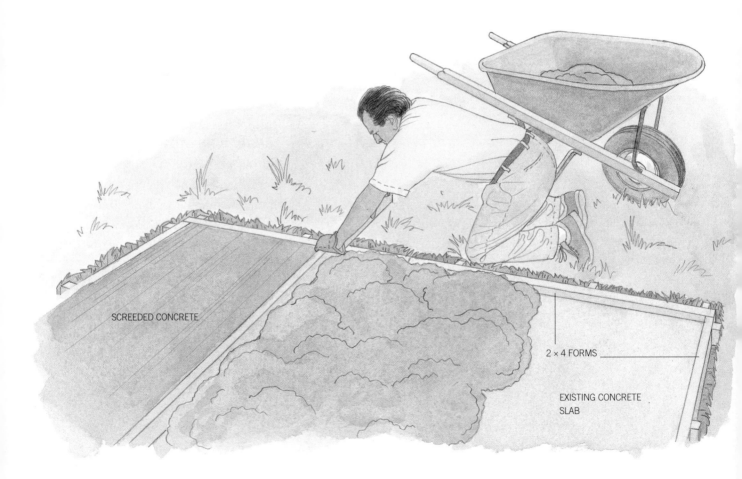

SCREEDED CONCRETE

2 × 4 FORMS

EXISTING CONCRETE SLAB

repairing concrete

A concrete crack can be simply filled with a concrete repair caulk. For a more permanent repair, first widen the crack using a hammer and cold chisel. "Key" the crack so that the bottom is wider than the top. Use a wire brush to dig out all the crumbs; then paint the inside of the crack with latex bonding agent. Mix a batch of vinyl patching concrete. Use a mason's trowel first to force the concrete into the crack, then to smooth the surface of the patch.

1 Prepare for Patching

Using a grinder or a circular saw equipped with a masonry blade, cut lines around a damaged area that are about ½ inch deep. Chisel out the area inside the cut lines, scrape away all loose materials, and paint with latex bonding agent.

2 Patch and Smooth

Mix a batch of vinyl concrete patch, trowel it into the repair, and smooth with a magnesium or wood float. Use a broom or steel trowel to match the finish of the surrounding concrete. Cover the repair with a sheet of plastic, and keep it moist for a week or so.

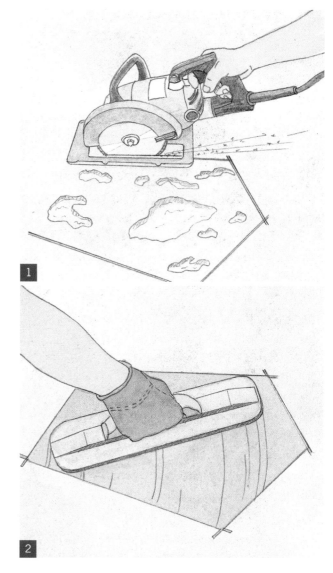

Patching an Outside Corner of a Step

If a step corner has cracked, cut around the damage with a grinder or circular saw equipped with a masonry blade. Chip away any loose material. If the damage is deeper than 3 inches, drive masonry screws to improve the bond. Then apply latex bonding agent. Make a simple form using a board and a heavy weight, such as a cement block. Fill the hole with vinyl concrete patch and trowel the surface. Remove the board as soon as the patch has started to harden, and smooth again.

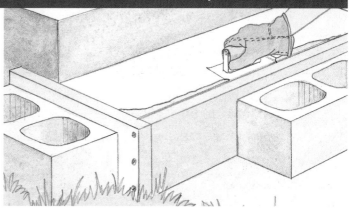

tiling over concrete

Before tiling a concrete slab, be sure it is stable; the tiles themselves will not add significant strength. Run a straight edge along the surface, and knock down any protrusions using a hammer and chisel or a grinder. Roughly patch large holes; small holes will be filled in when you trowel on the tile mortar. Apply a coat of latex bonding agent to the entire concrete surface.

These pages show how to install Mexican saltillo tiles, which are irregular in shape and size. To install quarry tiles or other tiles with standard shapes, use plastic spacers to maintain consistent grout lines.

1 Lay Out the Tiles

Often, saltillos and other large tiles are laid in 3-foot-square sections, each of which holds nine tiles. Test that this arrangement will lead to grout lines of the width that you want. Lay three tiles next to each other on a flat surface, spaced as you would like them to be in the finished installation. Measure the width of the three tiles and add the width of one grout line; this is the size of the squares in which the tiles should be laid. Using a tape measure and chalk line, mark lines in either direction to produce a grid of squares.

2 Trowel on Mortar

Mix a batch of latex-reinforced mortar. It should be just stiff enough to cling for a second or two to a trowel held vertically. Using a notched trowel of the size recommended by the tile dealer, spread the mortar inside one of the squares. First spread a thick layer using the flat side of the trowel. Then use the notched side to comb the surface of the mortar only; the notches should not scrape the concrete. Work to create an even surface with no globs or gaps.

3 Place and Align the Tiles

Set each tile straight down into the mortar; avoid sliding a tile more than $\frac{1}{2}$ inch. Position nine tiles in the grid. Stand up and examine the tiles from several angles to be sure that the grout lines are as consistent and straight as possible.

4 Bed the Tiles and Check Adhesion

Gently tap the tiles with a rubber mallet and a block of wood to embed them in the mortar and create a smooth tile surface. Every so often, pick up a tile to make sure the mortar is sticking to at least three-quarters of the back surface. If not, back-butter each tile with a thin layer of mortar before setting it in the troweled mortar.

5 Cut Tiles to Fit

Soft tiles like saltillos are cut using a rented wet saw, or a grinder or circular saw equipped with a masonry cutting blade. It will take several passes to cut halfway through the tile; then you can snap it to finish the cut. Other tiles can be cut more easily using a snap cutter; ask your tile dealer which cutting tool to use.

6 Grout and Clean

Wait for the mortar to harden completely; this may take two days. Mix a batch of latex-reinforced sanded grout. The mix should be fairly stiff—just to the point where it does not pour readily.

Holding a laminated grout float nearly flat, push grout between the tiles in at least two directions at all points. Tilt the float up, and squeegee away most of the excess grout. Drag a wet towel over the area; then wipe lightly with a damp sponge. You will need to rinse the sponge often. Once the grout starts to stiffen, use the sponge to create grout lines that are consistent in depth. Allow the grout to harden; then buff the surface with a dry cloth.

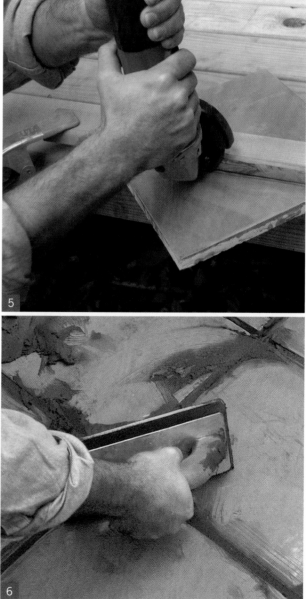

laying pavers on concrete

Use this technique to lay either natural bricks or concrete pavers. If you choose, you can install wood edging around the perimeter of the slab, and use the edging as a guide for screeding.

Check that the concrete slab is stable. Knock down any high spots with a hammer and chisel or a grinder, and apply latex bonding agent.

1 Spread the Mortar
Install permanent edging or temporary screed guides around the perimeter of the slab. The top of the edging should be the thickness of a paver plus ⅜ inch above the slab. Make a screed out of a 2 × 4 and plywood (see page 58); when the screed is resting on the edging or guides, it is ½ inch above the slab.

In a wheelbarrow, combine a bag of mortar mix with a shovel of Portland cement, and mix with water to achieve a mortar that is just thick enough to stick to a trowel that's held upside down for a few seconds. Shovel the mortar onto the slab, and smooth it out with the screed guide.

2 Set the Bricks
Using scraps of ½-inch plywood as spacers, set the pavers in the mortar. (The pavers will settle down ⅛ inch or so into the mortar when you install them.) You may be able to minimize cutting of pavers by allowing them to extend over the slab by an inch or so. Place a flat board on top of the bricks, and tap with a hammer to bed the bricks and ensure a flat surface.

3 Fill the Joints with Mortar
Once the mortar has dried, fill a grout bag with the same type of mortar. Squeeze the bag to squirt mortar into the joints. Once you have completed a 5-foot-square section, use a jointer to finish the joints, just as you would for a brick wall (see page 115).

Chapter Five

building walls

A freestanding wall can bestow privacy, frame a view, or define areas in a yard. Retaining walls hold soil in position or form the structure for garden beds. For either type of wall, you can use brick, block, stone, adobe, or landscaping timbers. In general, wall building calls for more patience, skill, and artfulness than patio construction. So take your time. Practice throwing mortar before you start to install a brick or block wall. When building a stone wall, expect to use up hours experimenting with various configurations before you find the one that suits your needs best. Stuccoing and facing a wall similarly call for artful consideration and practice. The time will be well spent, yielding a structure that is durable and uniquely your own.

Retaining walls
made of mortared
rubble keep the land-
scape firmly in place.
Building a wall with
large, rough stones
is slow, difficult work,
although the result
can be well worth
the effort.

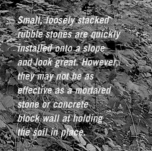

Small, loosely stacked rubble stones are quickly installed onto a slope and look great. However, they may not be as effective as a mortared stone or concrete block wall at holding the soil in place.

Ashlar stones stack almost as neatly as brick or block, yet have a more rustic appearance. If you mortar the stones and then rake the joints, the wall will be strong, yet look as though it was dry-laid.

Pressure-treated 6 × 6 timbers form retaining walls that are admirably incorporated into a deck and small set of stairs.

Below: This brick wall only looks haphazard. Although the bricks below follow a wavy course, the top of the wall is nearly flat.

A rustic stone-and-brick structure takes on the look of an ancient ruin. Artful plantings make it a bucolic setting.

A stuccoed wall provides solid privacy that is softened by overhanging plants. The short brick wall steps the lawn down gracefully and provides a backdrop for flowers.

Tawny dry-laid flagstones form a stunning circular planter. The shape, like the large, mortared cap stones, lends strength as well as beauty.

Foliage of any color looks great with a backdrop of natural brick. Efflorescence—a white powder caused by moisture—actually adds to the effect. A large brick structure like this is definitely a job for pros.

Above: A large decorative pillar adds a distinctly classic look to this brick garden wall.

Right: Landscaping timbers in this retaining wall have turned gray and developed splotches of green mildew, so that the wall mirrors the stones of the walk and picks up some of the plant colors.

Gray and brown ashlar stones form graceful curves in this entryway.

stacking blocks for a retaining wall

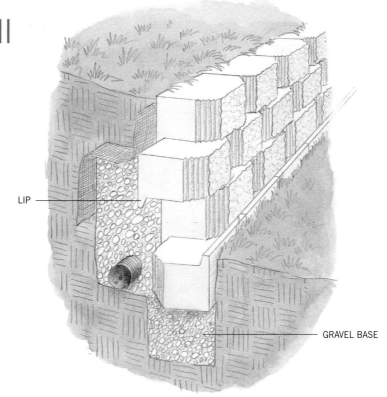

Home centers and brickyards carry several styles of concrete blocks shaped so that they will interlock when stacked to form a strong retaining wall. The wall will "batter" back, meaning that it will lean toward the soil that it retains. The blocks have a decorative face. Use a stackable retaining wall to keep a slope from eroding, or stack the blocks 2 or 3 feet high to make a flower bed.

Most stackable blocks have a lip at the rear bottom, which slips over the top back edge of the block below it. Others anchor via grooves or even fiberglass pins.

LIP

GRAVEL BASE

EXCAVATE AND LAY GRAVEL

There are three basic excavation options. One is to cut into the face of a hillside to create a vertical surface that slopes slightly backward. Depending on the height of the wall and condition of the soil, this could be difficult work. A second is to build the retaining wall at the bottom of the slope, then fill in behind it with gravel and soil. A third choice is to combine the first two methods by excavating about halfway down the slope. This way, you can use the excavated soil to fill in behind the retaining wall.

Lay out the site using stakes and mason's line if you want a straight wall. For a curved wall, lay out with a garden hose and sand (see page 27).

After any excavating of the slope, dig a trench 6 inches wider than the blocks and 6 inches deeper than the blocks' thickness. Fill the trench with compactible gravel, and tamp it with a hand tamper or a 4 × 4. For additional stability, rent a vibrating plate compactor (see page 39).

LAY THE BLOCKS

Set the bottom row of blocks upside-down and backwards, so the lips face up at the front. Check for level, and adjust the blocks as needed by adding or removing gravel from under them. Lay the second and third rows right side up; then fill in behind the blocks with gravel.

Continue stacking and filling until you have laid the blocks that will be second to the top. Using a caulk gun, apply several squiggles of construction adhesive, and set the top blocks in the adhesive (shown above). Spread landscaping fabric on the gravel, and fill in behind the top blocks with soil.

Drainage for Heavy Rainfalls

Because stackable blocks are not mortared in place, excess rainwater will seep through the joints between them and dribble out the front of the wall. If you expect heavy rain, or if water often flows down the slope that the wall is to retain, install drainage as shown on pages 36–37. Excavate a space about 16 inches wide behind the wall. After laying the first two courses of blocks, lay 2 to 3 inches of loose (non-compactible) gravel, sloped at a rate of at least $\frac{1}{4}$ inch per foot toward the area where you want excess water to flow. Lay a perforated drainpipe on the gravel, check again for slope, and cover with more gravel. Keep adding gravel as you build up the wall. Near the bottom of the topmost block, lay landscaping fabric on the gravel and cover it with soil.

working with mortar

An experienced bricklayer can "throw" a neat line of mortar, just the right thickness, with ease. Even if you are very handy, it would take months of practice to become that proficient. But, if you practice throwing mortar on a concrete or brick surface for couple of hours, you can learn to throw mortar well enough to construct a straight wall with neat joints. You will work much more slowly than a pro would, but the end result will be a masonry project that you can point to with pride.

Buy bags of mortar mix, which is cement mixed with sand. If the label reads "commercial grade,"

or is listed as type N, S, or M, it is strong enough for most outdoor projects. Consult with your supplier to be sure.

If it is convenient, you can scoop mortar directly out of the wheelbarrow with the trowel. Often, however, it is easier to load a shovelful of mortar onto a hawk or a piece of plywood about 16 inches square and work from there.

The techniques on this and the following page are shown for a typical brick wall. For details on planning the wall and positioning the bricks, see pages 112–115.

1 Mix and Test the Mortar

Into a wheelbarrow, pour a small amount of mortar mix—about one-third of a bag. (You can mix larger batches as you become more proficient.) Add water a little at a time, and mix with a hoe or a mason's hoe. Avoid overworking the mortar.

Mortar is thick enough when you can cut ridges in it with a mason's trowel and the ridges hold their shape. It is too dry if it appears crumbly. As another test, scoop up some mortar with a mason's trowel, and hold it upside down. The mortar should stay stuck for a second or two. If the mortar is too dry or too wet, add water or dry mix as needed.

2 Throw a Line

Scoop up mortar with the trowel. With the face of the trowel pointing up, give it a quick downward snap. The mortar will lift very slightly and make a light smacking sound as it settles back onto the trowel. This loosens the mortar's grip on the trowel.

Next comes the tricky part. To throw a line of mortar, extend your arm so the trowel is at the point farthest from you. Rotate the trowel until mortar starts to slide off, and pull it back toward yourself. The goal is to deposit mortar in an even line about 1 inch thick, three-quarters of a brick wide, and two or three bricks long. The process should be smooth and fluid, and take only a second or two; don't try to micromanage the throw.

3 Furrow the Mortar

Turn the trowel upside down and drag its point through the mortar to produce a channel about half the thickness of the mortar line. Take care that you do not cause mortar to slide off the side of the bricks. If excess mortar does slide onto the bricks below, slice it off in the same manner as shown in step 6.

4 Butter a Brick End

Every brick except the first one in a course needs to have at least one end buttered. Hold the brick in one hand, and load the trowel with a small amount of mortar. Slide the trowel at a 45-degree angle to the brick end and lightly pull the trowel back to butter the mortar onto the brick.

5 Push a Brick into Place

Set the brick on the mortar bed, about 2 inches away from the brick it will abut, and slide it into place. Ideally, a small amount of mortar will squeeze out of all the joints. A small gap in the joints can be filled when you strike the joint (see step 7, page 114). If there are gaps greater than an inch in either direction, remove the brick and start again.

If a brick sits too high, tap it down using the handle of the trowel. If it is too low, do not pull it upward; that would create a weak joint. Remove the brick, scrape off the mortar, and start again.

6 Slice Off the Excess

Use the trowel like a knife to slice off the squeezed-out mortar. If you do this quickly and in one motion, little mortar will smear onto the face of the bricks.

Every 10 minutes or so (depending on the heat and humidity), go back and strike the joints and perhaps clean the joints; see page 114. Stop when the mortar starts to harden.

building a brick garden wall

The bricklaying techniques shown here are some of the most tried-and-true methods in all of construction. They have remained essentially the same for many centuries.

To make a story pole (step 5, page 114), lay a number of bricks on edge on a flat surface, with ³⁄₈-inch spaces between them. Then lay a length of 1 × 2 or 1 × 4 next to the bricks, and draw marks indicating the centers of each mortar joint. Alternatively, purchase a ready-made story pole.

Any mortared wall must rest atop a solid concrete footing; see pages 88–89. Before you start laying bricks, practice the mortar techniques shown on pages 110–111. To cut bricks, see pages 54–55.

BOND CONFIGURATIONS

For strength, a freestanding brick wall must have two wythes (parallel, abutting walls of bricks). To increase the strength of a wall, some bricks should be turned sideways to tie the two wythes together; these bricks are called "headers." (Regularly laid bricks are called "stretchers.") Over the centuries, masons have developed patterns, called "bonds," most of which incorporate headers in a regular pattern.

In some areas, a brick wall may be required to have steel reinforcement. Check with your building department to see which bonds will be compatible.

RUNNING BOND has no headers, so it is not as strong as the others. It is suitable for low walls or for use as a veneer (a single-width wall set up against an existing wall). It can be strengthened by metal ties that run across the width of the wall.

FLEMISH BOND alternates headers and stretchers in each course. You'll need to cut closure bricks at corners.

ENGLISH BOND alternates courses of headers and stretchers. It also requires that you cut closure bricks at corners.

COMMON BOND, also known as American bond, is shown being installed on pages 113–114. It uses headers every fifth course, so it requires a small amount of extra cutting.

RUNNING BOND

CLOSURE BRICKS

FLEMISH BOND

CLOSURE BRICKS

ENGLISH BOND

CLOSURE BRICKS

COMMON BOND

1 Lay a Dry Run

Snap chalk lines on the footing indicating the outline of the wall. Place the bricks on the footing in a dry run, with ⅜- or ½-inch dowels between them to represent the joints. Make sure you understand how the bricks will be laid out at the corner; you may need to cut a brick or two. To minimize cutting, you may choose to adjust the thickness of the joints, or you may move one wall over an inch or so. With a pencil, mark the footing for the centers of each joint.

2 Lay the First Bricks

Remove the dry-laid bricks. Starting at a corner or the end of a wall, throw a line of mortar for the first three bricks, and butter the brick ends for all but the first brick (see pages 110–111). Push bricks into place, and use a level to check that they are level in both directions. Scrape away excess mortar. Repeat for the second wythe, and lay bricks for the start of an adjoining wall if you are at a corner.

3 Lay a Header Course

Be sure you understand how the bricks must be stacked and perhaps cut at the corners for the bond configuration you have chosen. For common bond, a header course needs 2 three-quarter bricks and 2 one-quarter bricks, known as closures, at the corner. If you need plenty of partial-size bricks, cut them factory style using a wet masonry saw.

4 Build a Lead

Continue building the corner or end of the wall, also called a lead. Make a stack 7 or 8 bricks high. The higher the lead, the longer it must be. As you go, use a level to check that the corner is plumb and that the courses are level. Use a story pole to see that joints are the correct thickness. Finally, use a level or other straightedge to see that the bricks form regular "stair steps" at the unfinished end.

5 String a Line Between the Leads

Build a lead at the other end of the wall in the same way as you built the first (step 4). Use the story pole to check that bricks in one lead are the same height as bricks in the other lead. Using line blocks, stretch a mason's line from one lead to the other, at the center of a joint. Be sure that the line is taut.

6 Fill In Between the Leads

Lay all the in-between bricks for the bottom course of both wythes, using the pencil lines as guides. Move the line blocks up one joint, and fill in the next course. The last brick in the middle of a course, called the closure brick, is buttered at both ends. Butter it generously, and slip it in straight down; avoid sliding it. You may need to force additional mortar into one of the joints with a striking tool.

7 Strike the Joints

Every 10 minutes or so, depending on weather conditions, stop laying bricks and strike the joints. If you wait until the mortar has started to dry or harden, striking will be difficult. Using the jointing tool of your choice (see opposite page), smooth all horizontal joints first; then smooth the verticals. If a bit of mortar oozes out the side of the jointing tool, resist the temptation to smear it while it is still wet.

8 Clean at the Right Time

As soon as the mortar has just started to harden (it will appear crumbly), wipe the joints lightly with a masonry brush. If the mortar smears, stop and wait a few minutes before trying again.

If mortar smears onto the bricks, you may be able to wipe it off with a damp sponge, but take care not to get the joints very wet, or you will weaken them. Alternatively, wait a day and then clean with a mild muriatic acid solution.

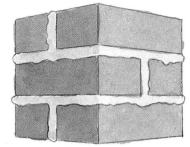

EXTRUDED JOINT

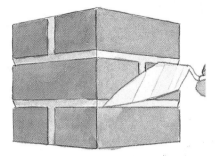

FLUSH JOINT

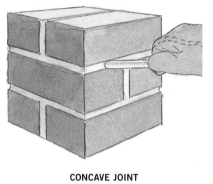

STRUCK JOINT

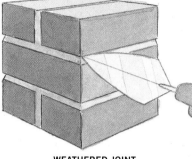

WEATHERED JOINT

RAKED JOINT

CONCAVE JOINT

CHOOSING A JOINT TYPE

Striking (or tooling) a joint shapes and compacts the mortar, increasing its strength and ability to shed water. If you have freezing winters, choose a joint that sheds water quickly, so frozen moisture cannot produce cracks.

EXTRUDED JOINT is simply squeezed-out mortar that has been left alone. It has a pleasing rustic appearance, but is not watertight.

FLUSH JOINT is produced by cutting mortar away, with no striking. The resulting joints are typically pitted and are suitable for dry, warm climates only.

STRUCK JOINT is produced by scraping with a trowel tilted upward. This produces dramatic shadow lines. The joint is compacted and fairly strong, but water can easily collect at the bottom.

WEATHERED JOINT is an upside-down struck joint. It is very watertight, and fairly strong.

RAKED JOINT, produced with a joint raker, can cast interesting shadows. It is not very strong, and has little resistance to water.

CONCAVE JOINT is the most common. Make it using a jointer. It sheds water nearly as well as a weathered joint, and does a good job of compacting the mortar.

CAPPING THE WALL

The top, or cap, of a brick wall is important to its overall appearance. If you plan to set flower pots or drinks on top, choose something wide, like limestone block. Set limestone in an extra-thick bed of mortar. A header course is laid in the same way as standard bricks. Capping a brick wall with more bricks creates a clean finished look (below). To install a rowlock course, you will need to butter the sides of each brick.

stuccoing a wall

Stucco covers imperfections in a wall, creating a blank slate that you can paint or decorate at will. It also softens the look of a wall, rounding edges and effecting a mellow appearance.

It may take you a couple of hours before you get the hang of stuccoing. Fortunately, the base coat—which you install at the beginning of your learning curve—will be covered up. Before applying the finish coat, practice on a vertical piece of plywood or an obscure portion of the wall. That way, when you start applying the final coat to a visible area, you will have developed habits and strokes that you can use on the entire wall to produce a surface that is consistent in appearance.

The masonry surface to be covered must be clean and dry. Wash away any surface oils using a degreaser. If a brick wall is flaking or has produced a dusty white powder called efflorescence, that means it's been wet for long periods. Remove the causes of the moisture, and clean with a 10 percent solution of muriatic acid.

1 Apply the First Coat
Paint the surface with latex bonding agent by following the manufacturer's instructions. Pour about half a bag of dry stucco base coat mix into a wheelbarrow. Add water and mix with a hoe or mason's hoe to produce a pasty consistency. The stucco should be just firm enough to hold its shape when you pick it up with a trowel.

Place a shovelful of stucco on a piece of plywood or a hawk. Hold the hawk against the wall as you work, so you can catch any drips. Scoop up the stucco with a straight finishing trowel, and slather it onto the wall, pressing it into place. Aim at a coat that has a uniform thickness of ⅜ inch.

2 Scarify the Base Coat
When the base coat has started to stiffen, comb the surface with a scarifying tool. Work to produce indentations, without raising crumbly ridges. For

maximum strength, take steps to ensure that the base coat cures slowly—ideally, for two days. Cover it with plastic, or spray it with a fine mist every few hours for two days.

3 Apply a Finish Coat

Mix stucco for the finish coat the same way as you did for the base coat, except that the mix should be slightly wetter. If you buy white stucco finish, you can mix it with dry colorant to achieve a long-lasting color that does not need to be painted. Apply the finish coat in the same way as the base coat.

4 Apply a Texture

To produce a travertine finish, generally smooth the surface. Then use a whisk broom or masonry brush to spatter the surface with globs of stucco. Knock the globs down a bit using a flat trowel.

5 Shape a Corner

When you come to an outside corner, hold a piece of 1 × 4 against the other wall as shown, and apply stucco up to the 1 × 4. Texture the stucco and allow it to partially set before stuccoing the other wall.

Stucco Textures

Stucco finishes reflect the personality of the worker. Follow one of these techniques, or develop a method of your own. The important thing is to maintain a consistent pattern throughout the job. Note the two different looks that were achieved on the walls above, just by the way the finish coat was applied.

facing a concrete or block wall

Another way to dress up a wall is to cover it with flagstones. Choose stones that are light and thin, making them easy to cut as well as to lift. They should be nearly flat as well. Heavy stones may pull away from the wall as you work.

The wall itself should be in sound condition. If a brick wall is flaking or producing a white powder called efflorescence, take steps to solve the problems before applying face stones (see page 116).

1 Lay the Stones in a Dry Run

Lay a sheet of plywood, as wide as the wall is high, on the ground near the wall, placing it so you can easily pick up stones from the plywood and apply them to the wall. Lay stones on the plywood in a dry run, mimicking how they will appear on the wall. Arrange them much as you would for a flagstone patio, cutting with a hammer and chisel where necessary (see page 54).

2 Apply Mortar to the Wall

Paint a coat of latex bonding agent onto the wall. In a wheelbarrow, combine a bag of commercial-grade mortar mix with a shovelful of Portland cement for added sticking power. Add water slowly and mix with a hoe or mason's hoe to achieve a mortar that is firm but wet enough to stick to the stones. Use a straight trowel to apply the mortar to the wall. Aim for a coat about $3/8$ inch thick (thicker if the stones are very uneven in shape). Cover an area of about 15 square feet. For heavy stones, only apply mortar to the lower part of the wall at first (see steps 3 and 4).

3 Set the Bottom Row of Stones

Starting at the bottom, press the stones into the mortar. Where necessary, use blocks of wood or small rocks to hold the stones in position.

5 Fill and Strike the Joints

Before the mortar has hardened, go back and fill in the joints with mortar. Use a pointed trowel or a mortar bag to slip and press mortar into the joints. Wipe the edges with a damp towel, which you will need to rinse often.

4 Set the Upper Stones

If the stones are light enough, you can simply continue setting stones up to the top of the wall. However, if the weight of the upper stones causes lower stones to slide down out of position, you may need to wait for the mortar to set for the lower stones before installing the upper ones. Continue to use spacers to maintain fairly consistent joints. Every 10 minutes or so, pull a stone off the wall and check the back to make sure at least three-quarters of it is embedded in mortar. If not, back-butter the stones with a thin coat of mortar before setting them.

6 Cap and Clean the Wall

At the top of the wall, install large stones that overhang the wall by an inch or more on either side. When the mortar has started to harden, wash the wall with water and a brush, and rinse with a wet towel. To clean smears or a general haze, use a 10 percent muriatic acid solution the next day.

building a dry stone wall

A stone wall calls for plenty of heavy lifting, so take it easy. Avoid stones that weigh over 50 pounds. Have the stones delivered as close to the site as possible, and enlist help. Take your time; you can stretch out a project like this over several weekends.

Choose stones that are at least partially squared off. Stones with a basically round shape are hard to stack firmly. You will need a good number of "tie stones" (also called "bond stones") long enough to span the thickness of the wall. Sort the stones into three or four piles, according to size. That will make it easier to find the stone you need. Reserve plenty of large stones to use for the wall's cap.

A batter gauge (shown in step 2, opposite page) enables you to check that the wall leans inward on both sides, so that the top is narrower than the bottom. Make one by taping a 4-foot 2 × 4 to a level, with an intervening scrap of wood at the top.

A Stone Retaining Wall

Stacked stones can hold back a 4-foot-high embankment, as long as they are assembled correctly. Batter the wall back at a rate of 1 inch per foot or more. Stack the stones with extra attention to stability; no stone should wobble, and each stone should span across a joint below. Every third or fourth course, set extra-long stones that extend 6 inches or more beyond the wall in the direction of the soil being retained. Fill the area behind with non-compactible gravel as you go. Excess rainwater will seep out the face of the wall.

1 Dig a Trench and Lay the First Stones

Remove sod and all other organic material from an area about 3 inches wider than the desired bottom thickness of the wall. Scrape rather than dig the bottom of the excavation, so the stones will rest on undisturbed soil. Check with a straightedge to see that the excavation is fairly flat. If the yard is not level, you may choose to dig a level excavation, in which case the bottom course will be horizontally out of alignment with the yard. Alternatively, follow the slope of the yard and build a wall that is slightly out of level.

Lay a tie stone at either end. Fill in with stones laid in two wythes. Fill spaces between the wythes with tightly packed stones.

2 Lay Additional Courses

As you continue to lay stones, aim to make the courses fairly level. Whenever possible, lay "one on top of two" rather than stacking stones of the same size directly on top of each other. Use the batter gauge to check that the wall leans inward slightly on either side. Every third or fourth course, install tie stones every 2 or 3 feet. If you need to cut stones, see page 54. Fill any large gaps by gently tapping in small stones.

3 Mortar the Cap Stones

Finish the top with large, flat cap stones that overhang the sides of the wall on either side. Set the cap stones in a 1- to 2-inch-thick bed of mortar. The mortar should not be visible.

building a mortared stone wall

A mortared wall must rest on a solid concrete foundation; otherwise, the mortar joints will crack. See pages 88–89 for pouring a footing. Make sure the foundation meets local codes, which reflect regional conditions.

Don't depend on the mortar to hold the wall together. Choose stones that are at least partially squarish and flat, so they can rest on top of each other without wobbling. Sort the stones into three or four piles according to size, to make it easier to find the stone you need. If the stones are dirty, clean them with a masonry brush and water; a dirty stone will not adhere well to mortar. If the stones are very porous, soak them in water just prior to installing them.

Make a batter gauge similar to the one shown on page 121. However, a mortared wall does not need to be as severely battered as a dry-laid wall. So build a gauge that allows a 4-foot-high wall to lean back about 2 inches.

1 Lay the First Stones on the Footing

Mix a stiff batch of commercial-grade mortar (see page 110). As you work, periodically check that the mortar is sticking to the stones. If the mortar starts to harden or get crumbly, throw it out and mix a new batch.

2 Lay Additional Stones

Set three or four stones much as you would for a dry stone wall (see pages 120–121). Check that they rest without wobbling, and always lay one on top of two, spanning a joint below. Remove the stones, keeping careful track of where they belong. Spread a 1-inch-thick bed of mortar, and set the stones back in position. Fill gaps larger than 2 inches with small stones rather than mortar. If a stone sinks down too deep in the mortar or wobbles, hold it up in one or two places by tapping in small wooden wedges. After the mortar stiffens, pull the wedges out and stuff the holes with mortar.

3 Rake the Joints

Check the mortar periodically for stiffening. Once you can press your thumb into the mortar and leave an impression without mortar sticking to your thumb, it's time to rake the joints. Hold a small scrap of wood at an angle, and run it along the joint lines so it compacts the mortar as you scrape away excess. Avoid smearing mortar onto the stones. Work to produce joints that are consistent in depth.

4 Brush and Clean the Wall

After raking, brush the joints with a masonry brush to remove all mortar crumbs. If a stone is smeared with mortar, dampen the brush or a small towel and scrub, taking care not to soak any nearby joints. Dried globs of mortar can be cleaned the following day by first chipping with a hammer and chisel and then washing with a 10 percent muriatic acid solution.

building a timber retaining wall

A timber retaining wall is a heavy-duty wall that can hold a hill firmly in place. If you use pressure-treated 6 × 6s rated for ground contact, it will last for a long time. The work is heavy-duty as well. Plan on many hours of digging and hauling soil.

If you have only a modest slope, or if you want to build a wall like this and backfill it with soil for a planting bed, you can omit the deadmen (see opposite page), which will make the work much easier.

Some rainwater will seep through the front of the wall. If you expect lots of rain, install a perforated drainpipe that slopes away from the site (see page 109), and perhaps leads to a dry well (see page 37).

To cut 6 × 6s, use a small square to mark a line on all four sides, cut the lines with a circular saw, and finish the cut using a handsaw or a reciprocating saw. Alternatively, cut with a chain saw if you are experienced in its use.

EXCAVATE AND INSTALL THE FIRST COURSE

Dig away the side of the hill to create a vertical surface that slopes slightly toward the hill. You may choose to excavate about halfway down the slope, and use some of the excavated soil to backfill the wall (see page 109).

Lay out for the base of the wall using stakes and mason's line. The wall should be at least close to level. Dig a trench 12 inches wide and 8 inches deep. Scrape rather than dig the bottom, so as not to disturb the soil. Pour and spread 3 inches of non-compactible gravel in the trench, and tamp it with a hand tamper or a piece of 4 × 4.

Cut 6 × 6s to fit; avoid having any pieces shorter than 6 feet. Set the first course in the trench, aligned with the mason's line. If necessary, remove or add gravel so that the boards form a continuous straight line and rest without wobbling.

Using a long drill bit, bore a ½-inch hole down through the boards every 3 feet or so. Cut pieces of ½-inch rebar to 3 feet (the length may vary, depending on soil conditions), and use a small sledge hammer to drive them down through the holes and into the ground (left).

BUILD THE WALL AND INSTALL DEADMEN

Stack the next course so it is set back ½ inch closer to the hill than the course beneath it. Drill pilot holes and pound 12-inch spikes every 3 feet or so, to attach the two courses together firmly.

When you reach the third or fourth course, construct deadmen, to be installed every 6 to 8 feet along the length of the wall. To do so, cut one timber to 6 feet and one to 3 feet. Place the pieces on a flat surface in the form of

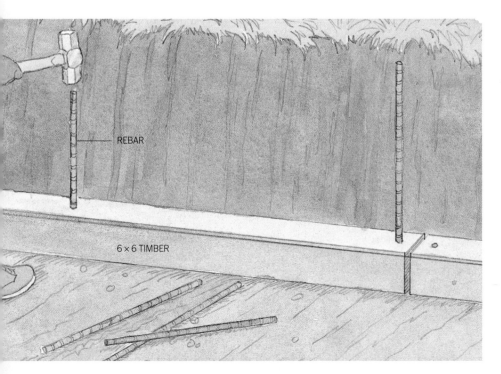

REBAR

6 × 6 TIMBER

a T. Drill pilot holes and drive two 10-inch galvanized lag screws to join the two pieces together.

Dig a T-shaped trench to accommodate each deadman (right). It may help to place a deadman on the hill where it will go, and slice around it with a shovel to mark for the excavation. Dig the sod carefully, so you can replace it after the wall is built.

Set a deadman in position, and check that it is fairly level. Drill pilot holes and drive two 12-inch spikes to attach the front of the deadman to the wall.

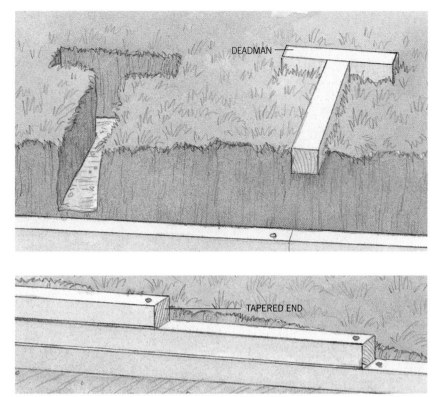

DEADMAN

TAPERED END

FINISH THE WALL AT THE ENDS

If the wall needs to taper at the ends, cut and install 6 × 6s in each course as long as they need to be to hold back the soil (as shown in the bottom illustration above). If the wall must turn a corner, alternate the courses as shown at left, and drive spikes both downward and into the sides of the timbers for a firm connection.

DEADMAN

credits

PHOTOGRAPHY CREDITS

Unless otherwise credited, all photographs are by **Frank Gaglione**.

Marion Brenner: 3 top, 78 bottom left, 103, 105; **Wayne Cable:** 96, 97; **Gary Conaughton:** 93; **Crandall & Crandall:** 25, 75 bottom right, 107, 117 bottom left; **Robin Cushman:** 2; **R. Todd Davis:** 78 middle right, 108; **Alan & Linda Detrick:** 1, 44 bottom, 47 bottom, 102 top; **Roger Foley:** 4, 13 left, 41, 64 bottom, 99, 118 top; **Philip Harvey:** 80; **Saxon Holt:** 44 top, 52, 78 middle left, 90 top, 92 left, 92 right, 120 bottom; **Charles Mann:** 5 top, 6 top, 16 top, 45, 66, 101 bottom, 102 bottom, 104 top, 122; **Terrence Moore:** 10 bottom, 20, 48 bottom, 79; **Jerry Pavia:** 5 middle, 7, 12, 14 right, 15, 17 top, 17 bottom,

18 top, 18 bottom, 19 bottom, 40, 42, 46, 49, 50 top, 64 top, 71 bottom, 77 right, 78 bottom right, 101 top, 104 bottom, 106, 115; **Norman A. Plate:** 126; **Susan A. Roth:** 3 bottom, 8 right, 9, 43 top, 48 top, 71 top, 74 top, 74 bottom, 78 top, 100, 120 top; **Courtesy of Smith & Hawken:** 69 bottom right; **Michael S. Thompson:** 43 bottom, 47 top, 53 top, 91 bottom, 117 bottom right; **Tom Wyatt:** 90 bottom, 91 top

DESIGNER CREDITS

Julia Berman: 16 top; **Elspeth Bobs:** 122; **Terri and Ralph Cammicia:** 5; **Bob Clark:** 3 top, 6 top, 102 bottom, 103, 105; **Clinton & Associates:** 4, 118 top; **Concrete Solutions:** 93 bottom; **Connie Cross:** 3 bottom, 9 top, 43 top, 71 top, 120 top; **Pam Duthie:** 48 top; **Florence Everts:** 64 bottom; **GAYNOR Landscape Architects/Designers, Inc.:** 80; **Kristen Horne:** 74 top; **Gordon Kurtis:** 126; **Leigh Link:** 100; **Tom Mannion:** 13 left; **Steve Miller, Concrete Art:** 93 top right; **Oehme, Van Sweden and Associates:** 99; **Sharon Osmund:** 52; **Pam Panum:** 2; **Tom Pellett:** 74 bottom; **The Plantage:** 78 top; **Dean Riddle:** 1, 44 bottom; **Sarah and Lance Robertson:** 43 bottom, 53 top; **Rogers Gardens:** 107; **Ardie Runkel:** 47 bottom; **Robert Schultz:** 41; **Lane Williams Architects:** 80; **David Yakish:** 92 right

ACKNOWLEDGEMENTS

We would like to thank the following businesses for their help in supplying tools and materials: AJ's Contractor's Supply, Paso Robles, CA; Air Vol Block, Inc., San Luis Obispo, CA; Ocean Avenue Hardware, Cayucos, CA; Sanford Stone Company, Templeton, CA; San Luis Soils & Sod Farm, Los Osos, CA; Santa Barbara Stone & Masonry, Inc., San Luis Obispo, CA; Tileco, San Luis Obispo, CA; and Totally Tile Inc., Paso Robles, CA.

Index

Page numbers in **boldface** refer to photographs.